Cycle of Hope:

A Journey from Paralysis to Possibility

TRICIA DOWNING

Cycle of Hope: My Journey From Paralysis to Possibility

By Tricia Downing

1. Biography & Autobiography : Specific Groups – Special Needs

2. Sports & Recreation : Cycling – General 3. Health & Fitness : Physical Impairments

ISBN: 978-0-9819510-7-2

Cover design by Stacey Lane

Printed in the United States of America

Authority Publishing

11230 Gold Express Dr. #310-413

Gold River, CA 95670

800-877-1097

www.AuthorityPublishing.com

Always believe!

For those who have accompanied me along the way...

"...suffering produces endurance,
and endurance produces character,
and character produces hope
and hope does not disappoint us."

—Romans 5:3-5

PART I
SUFFERING

"Suffering is but another name for the teaching of
experience, which is the parent of instruction
and the schoolmaster of life."

—Horace

Chapter 1

It all happened so quickly. The realization. The impact.
The wind knocked out of me. And then screaming from above. I
couldn't see the faces, but I could feel the tension in the air. What
just happened?

I lay on the ground, flat on my back, unable to move.
Nothing was there holding me down, but when I tried to get my
legs to bend, my quads to tighten, or my ankles to roll—nothing
happened.

Two women rushed to the scene and kneeled over me as I
looked up from the ground, fear rushing through my veins. I was
fighting against the pain and shock as one asked, "What is your
name?"

With barely a breath, I whispered, "Trish."

As I was focused on answering the question, the other

woman bent down and began to unfasten my helmet.

"No! Don't do that!" I said with as much force as I could muster.

The first woman went back to her line of questioning. "What day of the week is it?"

"Sunday," I whispered.

"What is your friend's name?"

"Matt."

She continued, "What color is your bike?"

That sent me into a tailspin. *My bike*, I thought. *My brand-new red and yellow bike*. It was my prized possession.

Earlier that morning I had been looking forward to showing off my four-month-old Giordana racing bike. Matt, a friend from my racing circle, was visiting from out of town. Instead of spending the day touring the city's landmarks and museums, we decided to go for a fifty-mile bike ride so he could enjoy the natural beauty of the city of Denver. The details of what happened next were slowly filtering through my mind.

It was a sunny day in autumn. The date was September 17, 2000, and instead of making preparations to ease into the cold of another winter, my life was in bloom. I had just returned from a summer of adventure and excitement, started a new job and was in the best physical condition of my life.

From my house, we rode down side streets, playing "dodge the obstacles" as we maneuvered around parked cars and pedestrians. Once we reached the bike path, we were able to ride side-by-side. We reminisced about the summer and the fun we had racing in Wisconsin and at a stage race in Pennsylvania. We talked about our plans for the new year and how we would come back stronger and more focused than ever in the coming season.

Eventually, the bike path ended and we were back on the road, heading for the suburbs. We rode in single file again, until I felt my bike becoming sluggish and bumpy. I looked behind me and saw that I was riding on a flat. "Not again!" I exclaimed. I had fixed a flat earlier that morning.

"Do you want to turn around?" Matt asked. "Maybe this isn't your day."

"No, it's okay. I'll fix it. Let's keep going."

Since Matt wanted to see Denver, I was going to show him Denver. I wanted him to get a taste of the hills and the Colorado elevation. I thought that what he needed was a challenge and I wasn't going to be defeated in my attempt to impart the pain. A flat tire wasn't going to stop our ride.

We finished riding through town until we got to Golden, and the foot of our destination—Lookout Mountain. We settled in our saddles and began our climb to 7,500 feet.

As we ascended Lookout, the city faded below. The road curved back and forth like a snake in a series of switchbacks. As we climbed, the road below, the houses, cars and all of civilization became miniature. The air got cooler as we peddled along the tree-lined ribbon of road. Even though the climb is only four miles long, it felt as though we had ridden miles out of town. Finally, we reached the top of the mountain climb and felt the satisfaction of yet another small achievement on the bike. It was one of many workouts to challenge our bodies and build our fitness. Cycling is an adrenaline rush. It's addictive. And each workout, although at the time it may break you down, ends with a feeling of accomplishment and the reward of increased physical gain.

As I looked down over the city and across to the mountains, I felt like I was on top of the world. The only thing I could see in front of me was possibility. I felt, in that moment, invincible.

Heading down the mountain was our reward after the push and strain of riding to the top; though the journey down the winding and narrow hill isn't for the faint of heart. It's a roller coaster, a collection of dips and turns—and the added danger of a road open to cars. One wrong move could mean disaster. The descent requires one hundred percent attention at every moment and in every curve, but it's a rush to exceed twenty miles an hour with the wind kissing every part of your body and your brain fully engaged in the process of leaning, turning and keeping the bike upright.

As we reached the bottom, the air was fresh against our skin, and we basked in the glow of our ability to feed the fire inside us—to ride and be fit. I felt an exuberance I had never felt before. My bike was my freedom.

All of that changed in a brief instant. I remember the details of the accident as a slow motion movie in my head. We were returning home, riding east on 32nd Avenue in Golden almost a straight shot back into town. A car appeared on the other side of the road, heading west—toward us. The car maneuvered into its left turn lane. At that very moment, Matt and I were at the edge of an intersection with a side street—32nd and Crabapple. We were beginning to cross over Crabapple at the very same moment the car was accelerating through the turn lane and entering the same side street from 32nd. We had the right-of-way, so in that moment, we weren't considering that there could be a car coming in our direction. I entered the intersection as Matt was approaching the middle of the road. I was just far enough behind him to see him make a big swerving motion around the car to avoid being hit.

A wave of relief washed over me. *For sure the driver realizes we're here now*, I thought to myself about the near-miss. But then I realized that the driver had no idea that there were two cyclists on the road. I was far enough behind Matt to see what was happening, but not far enough to do anything about it. I went for the brakes, but it was too late. I crashed into the front corner of the car, soared into the air, turning, and slammed my back into the car's windshield. Rolling off the car after the impact and lying at the edge of the road, I felt as though my body were disconnected. My legs felt like they were floating in mid-air. It didn't feel right. In fact, it felt horribly wrong. I couldn't feel anything below my waist.

The sound of sirens brought me out of my daze and back to the present. I struggled for breath. I knew it was bad. Very bad. I wondered if I could be dying. In the background, I could hear that Matt was in a panic too, screaming at the driver. He was probably in shock. I knew he didn't see the accident, but I was sure he had heard it.

Swiftly, yet delicately, the paramedics encircled my neck with a brace, slid a backboard beneath me, shifted me onto a gurney and loaded me into the ambulance. A rush of commotion swarmed around me. Paramedics were taking my vital signs and firing questions and demands at me.

"What happened?"

"Can you wiggle your toes?"

"Can you feel me touching your leg?"

"How long of a ride were you on?"

"Did you see the car coming?"

I answered the best I could, but it felt like there was a stack of books sitting on my chest and a knife digging into my back. I was short of breath and anxious about what would happen next. I couldn't look to my left or right because of the confinement of the neck brace. All I could do was look straight up.

In my head I made silent bargains with God.

Please don't let this be something that can't be fixed, I pleaded. *Let me ride again.*

Chapter 2

At the hospital things moved even more quickly. The paramedics simultaneously barked medical terms and conditions, while rolling me out of the ambulance and into the hospital. The trauma team gathered around me, taking notes, assessing my injuries and pushing me into my own curtained-off cubicle in the emergency room.

Matt sidled up beside the gurney. "Go call my mom and tell her we're at St. Anthony Hospital." I whispered the number into his ear.

Before I knew it, Matt was by my side again. "I couldn't remember your mom's number, so I just called your brother Andy. He said he would make some calls and be right over."

The trauma team shooed Matt out of the way and went to work, prepping me for the series of examinations that were to follow. Large shears sliced through my cycling outfit. I knew they must have been cold, but I felt nothing as they glided along my skin. The staff continued undressing me, even removing my earrings and snipping out my belly-button ring.

My brothers Andy and Greg were the first to arrive. They entered the room together as if they were feeding off each other for support. "Sorry," Andy said in a soft, gentle voice. "We got held up at check-in. They needed us to help fill out some hospital forms. I called Mom and Fred and they are on the way. Can you tell us what happened?"

I filled them in on the accident. I knew every detail. I was conscious the whole time.

"I'm in a lot of pain," I told them as I fought back tears.

News spread quickly, and one by one, my family arrived at the hospital as they received the phone message relayed by Matt to Andy. Matt, who was in town just for the weekend and was due to leave in twelve hours, greeted each of them as they arrived. They were all strangers to him, but he couldn't avoid making their acquaintances and telling the story over and over, answering their barrage of questions. He was the only one who could give the true first-person account, and even then, he hadn't seen the accident, which happened ten feet behind him.

As I listened to him relate the tale, I realized I had been right. He had heard it. He had heard my bloodcurdling scream. He had heard the thump of my body as it ricocheted from the car to the ground. And he had seen the aftermath of the collision. He had seen me lying broken on the pavement. He had heard me gasping for breath.

I felt so small lying on the gurney, covered in crisp white sheets when my mom walked in. I experienced a rush of relief at the sight of her. It didn't matter that I had turned 31 six weeks before the accident. A mom is a mom no matter how old you are, and at that moment, I realized just how much I needed her. It was like I was back in the fifth grade when I broke my arm at gymnastics practice. At the time, I thought my world would come crushing down because it happened in May, just before the pool opened for the summer. With a cast on my arm, I wasn't going to be able to swim. As my mom and I sat in the hospital emergency room that night, I remember her holding me on her lap, smoothing my hair and consoling me through the trauma of it all.

This was a different time and a much more serious injury, but my need for her was just the same. I locked eyes with her and said, "Momma, I don't want to be paralyzed." Tears rolled down my cheek.

"Honey, don't worry," she soothed as she once again ran her fingers across my forehead and through my hair. "We don't know anything for sure yet."

But I *knew*. I couldn't feel my legs. I was paralyzed. I could see from her face that she was fighting that fear too. She looked like she wanted to take me in her arms and tell me that everything was going to be alright. But it wasn't going to be that easy. We both knew we were in for a lot worse.

"Honey," she said. "There's always hope. You must have

hope."

Hope. How ironic. When I was born they named me Hope. Don't ask me who "they" were—I don't know. It could have been the college kids who had an "oops" one night and knew they couldn't keep me. Or maybe the secretary at the Department of Welfare who had to fill out my paperwork and figured I would need all the positive energy I could get. Whoever it was, how could they have known that what I needed right then, lying in that hospital, was hope?

Before I came along, my mom, Patricia, Pattie for short, had given birth to three adorable boys. From the top of their tow-heads to the tips of their chubby pink toes, they were all born healthy and full of personality. And Mom loved them with all of her heart.

But something was missing. My mom wanted a girl—a baby to dress in ruffles and lace. A daughter to watch through the years, grow from toddler to teen and experience the life events of prom, graduation and marriage. She wanted that bond that can only be shared by mother and daughter. For my mom, the family would not be complete without a little sugar and spice. Maybe that's not the dream of every father, but Dad already had his boys. She yearned for a girl.

One day, Mom found an article in the *Rocky Mountain News*, "Alone in the World," about a little girl named Rene, who was up for adoption. The article read: "Rene is just six weeks old, but she already has a winning personality. She loves to be cuddled and shows curiosity about her surroundings. Because

Rene is of Negro-Caucasian descent it is difficult to find a home for this baby. She is one of about 50 children of special needs who have no prospects for adoption according to Denver Department of Welfare social workers." There was an address and contact person listed at the bottom of the article.

At that time in the late sixties, there was an abundance of mixed-race children up for adoption. It was still a period when people of different races weren't encouraged to be together, a time when these relationships could even be considered taboo. When a child came along, often the mother felt the only choice was to give the child up for adoption. There were enough of these cases that the Department of Welfare placed ads in the newspaper touting particular children who needed caring families and stable homes.

Mom clipped out the article on Rene and made up her mind. She was going to adopt a mixed-race baby. A girl! The more she thought about it, the more the idea appealed to her. She knew there were a lot of mixed-race babies out there who needed a home, and she liked the idea of being able to give one of those children a second chance. She also knew that if she wanted to have a fair-skinned child, she and Dad were capable of taking care of that themselves. As luck would have it, she had recently taken a course at the local women's college on Black History and found herself fascinated with the trials, tribulations and strength of the African American culture. Of everyone I know, my mother is one of the most kind and accepting people I have ever met. I used to tease her that she could strike up a conversation with a tree. She's not afraid to talk to anyone and she always takes an interest in what people say. She wants to know who they are and what makes them tick. She genuinely cares. And she doesn't discriminate. For Mom, race wasn't an issue. She just wanted a girl. A beautiful, brown baby girl.

She talked it over with Dad and soon they were filling out the forms. They went through family interviews with Social Services and put in their request for the type of baby they wanted. My mom's only stipulation was that she wanted a baby girl who was between two and six months old. My father, an obstetrician, had a great deal of knowledge about healthy versus unhealthy babies and was more concerned about the mother and her health history.

By the time my parents had completed the screening, baby Rene had already been adopted. But that didn't stop Mom. After starting the process in the heat of the July sun, six months later, in the dead of winter, my parents received the call. A five-and-a-half-month-old baby girl named Hope was waiting for them to take her home and love her. The entire Downing clan– including the boys, Sam, Andy and Greg– piled into the car and were on their way.

That was the day they met me. It wasn't a ceremonious exchange, but more like, "Here's the little girl you ordered." The cost of the entire adoption was in the neighborhood of twelve dollars—a fact my older brother Greg never lets me forget. His favorite insults when we were growing up were, "You didn't even cost as much as Barbie's penthouse!" or "I hope Mom and Dad kept the receipt!"

My mother fell in love with me instantly. She loved my olive skin and my deep chocolate-brown eyes. She loved the little tuft of curly black hair that stood straight up on the top of my head.

After Dad went back to work at the hospital that day, she took me to the hairdressers, then to the church to show me off. I didn't look anything like her or Dad, but Mom didn't care. I was her baby girl and her late birthday present. I arrived six days after her 32nd birthday. And from that day forward, even though I wasn't physically a part of her, I became an everlasting piece of who she is—her second half. She is Patricia Carolyn. My name is Tricia Lynn.

* * *

After a full battery of tests, I was finally moved to a room in the ICU. My family followed me up there to meet the nurses and help me get settled in. My mom, stepdad Fred, Matt, Andy and Greg were all there. My oldest brother, Sam, was going to catch a flight from Arizona the first thing the next morning and my dad would drive in from Lamar, Colorado, where he lived, which was about four hours away. Andy, my very detail-oriented brother, started in on the to-dos. "We should probably get some calls out to your friends. Trish, who should I call first?"

I told him to call my best friend Lisa and then I said, "Um, can you call Albert?" Albert was a friend who I had met the previous year at the Hood-to-Coast race in Oregon. We were on a team together, arranged through an organization called

World T.E.A.M. Sports, which fielded teams for different athletic
events combining able-bodied and disabled athletes. Albert was a
quadriplegic and wheelchair athlete, and though we hadn't talked
for months, I felt better knowing there was someone I knew who
could understand what I was going through.

"Anything else you need?" Andy asked.

"Yeah, my toothbrush, a comb and Martha," I said.

As soon as I said I wanted Martha, Greg let out a howl of
pain and burst into tears. He ran out of the room.

Anyone who knows me well knows Martha. She is my oldest
friend, my companion, my confidante. She is a stuffed animal. A
monkey. Martha and I go way back. When my parents divorced
when I was seven, and my father was living with Barb, a new
girlfriend, Greg and I used to visit them on the weekends. They
didn't really have any toys at their house, but they had a nice
little collection of stuffed animals. Every time I went over there,
I gravitated to this light brown, soft, fuzzy monkey with gangly
arms and legs. I would play with it all day and sleep with it at
night, and they would literally have to remove it from my grasp
when I would leave on Sunday afternoon. Finally, on my eighth
birthday, my dad and Barb wrapped the monkey up in a trash
bag with a big red bow and gave it to me for my present. I was
elated and I named her Martha. She has slept with me almost
every night of my life since then. She has traveled across the
country, gone to summer camp, college and the Olympic Games.
She has been tortured, mostly by Greg, thrown down the laundry
chute, tossed into the rafters and hidden from me more times

than I can count. She has soaked up more tears and heard all the stories. Oh, if that monkey could talk.

That's what made Greg burst into tears and run out of the room. If I asked for Martha, things were serious.

The last thing I needed from Andy was to call the school where I was working. I had just started a new job and had been there less than three weeks when the accident happened. I hadn't even gotten to the part where I knew what I was doing, but I was responsible for placing high school juniors and seniors in internships for the semester, and I had students counting on me. I wanted to make sure that someone from the school could call me the next day, so I could fill them in on the progress I was making getting the kids placed. I also wanted to make sure they knew I would be back because I didn't want them giving my job away to someone else.

* * *

Monday morning brought another flurry of activity at the hospital. After a restless night, my family arrived back at the ICU to find out the next steps in my treatment. Of course, there was surgery to be scheduled and more details to be learned about the extent of my injuries.

My dad arrived after his drive from southeastern Colorado, and his first stop was to see the doctors. My dad is also a physician—albeit an obstetrician-gynecologist—but even though he didn't know about spinal cord injuries, he could talk doctorspeak and get the information that we needed to know.

After hearing the news, Dad took the family into a waiting room and explained the situation in a way only he can. My dad is a big fan of drawing pictures to explain medical terms and conditions. He would often do that for us as we were growing up to explain what he had done at work, when we would ask him. He is famous for drawing these diagrams on paper napkins in restaurants. I can't tell you how many fallopian tubes and uteruses he drew as part of a dinner conversation, left for unsuspecting waitresses to pick up after us.

"Tricia's spinal cord has been bent and now, instead of being a straight line, it resembles an S," he explained as he drew a picture. "They say the highest level of damage is at the fourth thoracic vertebrae and that she is paralyzed from the chest down. She will probably never walk again," he said, and then added the kicker, "Basically, her life is over."

Because of his profession, my dad has that way of distancing himself from the emotions and telling it like it is. He has learned to see the medical side, not the human side, even with his family. He was also working from his main experience with paralysis. When he was a kid, a neighbor friend was paralyzed jumping on a trampoline, circa 1945, and at that time, when little was known about living with spinal cord injury (SCI), people ended up in nursing homes and not living long or full lives. In his mind, I was that kid on the trampoline, and my life was over.

Fortunately, I had a small sliver of hope tucked away in

my back pocket. I had been through this situation before—only from a different perspective. I knew my life wasn't over. I didn't know about the dark days or the struggles ahead, but I had seen someone close to me emerge on the other side. I had a role model and inspiration. His name was Aldenys.

I knew from the first moment I laid eyes on him that I was attracted to him. Aldenys was so full of life. I could tell just by looking at him. His body was always in motion whether he was playing games, entertaining others with his jokes or demonstrating his adeptness at acrobatics.

It was my freshman year in college and we were outside in the courtyard at a "welcome to school" mixer for our dorm at the University of Vermont. The organizers of the social had planned it as an icebreaker and team building opportunity so that students would bond with the other residents on their respective floors.

Aldenys lived on our floor. It was evident from the beginning that we on the fourth floor had a special connection, and much of the credit was due to Aldenys' outgoing personality. He had the enviable ability to bring people together, make them laugh and create a circle of warmth.

Aldenys and I quickly became good friends. We were both gymnasts. Our favorite things to do together were to challenge each other to handstand-walking or standing back flip contests. Whoever could walk the farthest with feet reaching skyward or do the most standing back flips in a row, won.

Aldenys always had a piece of my heart. I would write my friends at home and tell them about the "dreamy" sophomore

I had met at school and how I fantasized that one day I would
marry him. I thought we made a perfect couple, except for the
small detail of height. He was a compact and muscular five-foot-
four and I was tall and thin at five-foot-ten. But our skin matched
perfectly. Not that I really cared. Even so, he had the most
gorgeous mocha-colored skin and chocolate-brown eyes. Every
time I saw him walk down the hall I'd get woozy and my knees
would go weak. And when he was shirtless, look out. His skin was
baby soft and begged to be touched. His smooth chest was free
of even a single hair. His muscles rippled, evidence of the many
hours he spent at the gym.

I remember the night I got the news that Kate, one of my
best friends from high school, had been killed in a car accident. As
soon as Aldenys heard, he swooped me into his muscular arms.
Even in my grief, I was aware of him. As I smelled his soft scent,
my heart skipped a beat.

Aldenys and I were not destined to be boyfriend and
girlfriend, but instead good friends. Even so, I took every
opportunity I could to spend time with him, whether it was alone
or in a group. Each time, my insides whirled with butterflies and
my head felt light and airy.

I still remember the day he got hurt my sophomore year. I
had just gotten home from a diving meet when the phone rang.
"Trish," the caller said urgently, "Aldenys is in the hospital. He
landed on his head at the gymnastics meet yesterday and broke
his neck. He's really hurt. They took him out on a stretcher."

I dropped my sports bag, tore down the stairs and flew out

the front doors of the dorm. I ran all the way to the hospital at the other side of campus. When I got there, I stopped at the front desk and asked for his room. On the ride up the elevator, I noticed that my palms were sweaty and my muscles were tensing up.

Slowly, I stepped into the room. Al was alone, lying on a bed that tilted back and forth. I inched over to the bed. "Al," I whispered so low I wasn't even sure the words came out of my mouth. "It's Trish."

"TTRRRIIISSSHHH," he replied. He used the same drawn-out expression of my name that he usually used, only this time it was quieter and more labored. I wanted to touch him, but I didn't dare. He looked so fragile. I was scared for him.

"I had a bad meet yesterday," he said light-heartedly, as if he had just stubbed a toe or something. A smile crept across his face.

"Umm, I can see that," I teased, following his lead.

"How was *your* meet?" he asked me.

"I had a bad meet too," I said. "I did a front two and a quarter to my face."

I could tell he was tickled by the vision of me kicking out of my flip too early and landing flat on my face in the water. On any other day, he would have teased me mercilessly. But not today.

"What happened, Al?"

"I was on the rings going for a double back dismount," he explained. "But you know how sometimes you get in the air and it doesn't feel right and you change your mind?"

Al had hesitated just enough and before he knew it, his

head hit the ground and his neck snapped. I didn't know what to say to him, so I just pulled up a chair and sat there. He didn't complain about pain or being hurt. He just calmly told me the events of the day, all the while maintaining his light mood.

Al would never walk again. I thought about him endlessly those first weeks I was in the hospital. I remembered how, when he was in the situation in which I now found myself, he tried to stay upbeat, even though I finally realized it was probably more for the benefit of his friends and visitors. I thought about the night I sneaked into his room way after visiting hours and had a heart-to-heart with him. He poured his emotions out and I got a glimpse into the hurt and difficulty he was experiencing. He left school for the next year and when I saw him again, he had made many strides toward getting back into life. He returned to school, drove a new van and was back to joking with his friends. On the outside he seemed okay. But it wasn't long before our paths parted, and I never saw him again. I was sure he would go on to live a positive and successful life. At least that's what I told myself because I needed his support, even though it had been fifteen years since I saw him last. He gave me the faith I needed to move forward. I knew he had been put into my life for a reason. Here it was. I would follow his lead. I would survive.

* * *

When my dad came into my room, my brother Sam, who is also a physician, was by his side. They looked down at me and

Dad said, "Hello honey, how are you doing?"

"I'm okay Dad," I said as light-heartedly as I could muster.

I turned my attention to my oldest brother. "When did you get in?"

"Just a little while ago," Sam answered. "We've just talked with the doctors and they say that your spinal cord is bent and bruised."

"The good news is that they don't think the spinal cord is severed," Dad explained.

"They're going to operate to stabilize your spine to prevent further injury," Sam added quietly.

As I listened to my brother explain the procedure, I fought to keep my eyes open. I wanted to stay awake. But the adrenaline had worn off and the intravenous morphine was beginning to take effect. I succumbed to sleep.

When I opened my eyes again, the room was darkened. A dim light above the head of my bed acted like a nightlight and chased the shadows into the corners of the room. I was getting tired of looking at the ceiling. I tried to move—to no avail. My legs were like dead weights below and my arms were restrained by my IV on one side and what I realized was a blood-pressure cuff on the other. I looked up and Matt was sitting in the corner of the room. "I'm thirsty," I told him.

"You still can't have anything to drink until they figure out when your surgery will be," he said.

Here it was Monday night and I hadn't had anything to drink since I took the last sip on my bike water bottle. I had ridden more than twenty miles, was dehydrated and still twenty-four hours later was not allowed to have a glass of water. It was torture. The only thing my nurse, Debbie, would allow me was to suck on a little sponge.

"Have you been here all day? Where did Dad and Sam go?"

"Your dad took us all out to dinner," Matt said. "He wanted to talk about your situation and what your family needed to do."

"What do you mean? Everyone was talking about what to do with me?" I felt defensive.

"It wasn't like that, but he was concerned about where you're going to live when you get out of the hospital and who would take care of you. Things like that."

"What do you mean *who is going to take care of me*? I can take care of myself!"

I hated that they were talking about me behind my back. While I was trying my hardest to be strong and hopeful, it seemed like they were preparing for my demise. In their eyes, I had become the guest of honor at a pity party—a charity case. I would no longer be able to make it on my own. I was thankful that Matt could be a spy for me. I knew he could tell me what the others couldn't. Like me, he was still keeping the door open for optimism.

In that moment—and, to be honest, in many others—I was happy to have Matt there with me. But that sentiment hadn't been true all weekend. In fact, before the accident, I had been counting the hours until Matt would just leave town.

Matt and I had known each other exactly nine weeks at the

time of my accident. In that amount of time, we had gone from the first meeting to flirting, courtship, love and the demise of our relationship.

So much happened in that span of time until I experienced my life-changing tragedy. But there was one other detail to add to the mix. That detail's name was Dave.

One month before I met Matt in Wisconsin, I met Dave. Since I was a teacher at the time, I had the great luck of having my summer off. I decided to spend the beginning of the summer in Colorado Springs, where I had lived previously, racing and training with friends. My plan was to hang out there for a few weeks and then hit the road and race as much as I possibly could. I had planned to take a four-week trip across the country to participate in some multi-day competitions and pretend to be a professional cyclist. I couldn't think of anything better than just riding all day, every day. My plan was to leave for the first series of races in Wisconsin at the beginning of July. In the meantime, I spent my days in the Springs, training with friends who were staying at the Olympic Training Center and racing at the velodrome, a special banked track for bike racing at high speeds.

That's when I met Dave. I don't remember the exact moment when I met him; I just remember him hanging around the velodrome during the Tuesday and Friday night races. When he wasn't riding, he would stand and watch the cyclists race round and round the 333-meter track. Every now and then I would catch a look at him. He had those great, cyclist legs and he was tall and handsome. He was in the Army so his sandy brown hair was cropped short, military style. Thin, black-rimmed glasses framed his soft eyes and he had the biggest, happiest smile that showed all of his teeth. Then, one day he asked me out.

I hadn't had a serious boyfriend in a couple of years, so I was excited at the prospect of meeting someone new. But I also knew that I didn't want to cancel my cross-country trip. Dave and I spent two weeks together getting to know each other, riding our bikes and hanging out at his house. He came along just as I wanted to be in a relationship, but while I liked him, I wasn't crazy about him. I liked the *idea* of being with him, though. He was the complete package. While he could fix my bike and challenge me on a ride, he could also whip up an amazing meal, keep a clean and tidy house and he was incredibly bright. On paper: perfect. In reality, he didn't light a spark, but I was willing to try. But that would have to wait until I got home from my trip.

Although I postponed my trip a couple of days to spend more time with Dave, I packed up my car and headed east on the seventh of July. My first stop was a series of races called Superweek, in Wisconsin. Superweek was two weeks' worth of one-day races, scattered across the state. Most of them were criteriums, which were my favorite. A criterium is a bike race on a closed-circuit course, usually about one to two miles per lap. They are generally timed, about forty-five minutes to an hour of high-speed racing.

Since there aren't as many female riders as there are men, the women's races only took place the second week of the event, while the men had two full weeks of racing. But I wanted to race both weeks, so I talked to the promoters and they said I was welcome to race with the men and just race down a category. So, I did. I raced three days with the men in several different spots near Milwaukee. I was traveling by myself, and stayed at a hostel for those nights, filling my days by watching the other races after mine had ended. One day, the race was on a beautiful course in Whitnall Park. When my event was over, I went back to the hostel to shower and then returned to the park to watch the pro races. As I was sitting there sunning myself, a good-looking guy with short, dark hair and piercing blue eyes came up to me and said, "Mind if I join you?"

"Uh, no...not at all," I stammered.

He introduced himself and said his name was Matt. He said, "I raced with you yesterday at the Proving Grounds. That's cool you're not afraid to race with the guys."

"Yeah, I didn't do so great, but it was fun. I'm looking forward to a little girl power next week, though," I said.

"It'll be better scenery for me next week, too," he said, and flashed a smile that showed his dimples.

We sat on the grass and talked the rest of the day. It was so easy to talk to him and we hit it off instantly. When he left, he told me he had to fly back home to Philadelphia for a wedding, but that he'd be back by the weekend. "Hopefully I'll see you at the other races?"

"Yep, I'll be here the rest of the series," I told him.

"OK...see you soon," he said. And like that, he was gone.

Two days later, I was on my way to a road race in Hartford,

Wisconsin. When I got there, all the women were already getting ready to head to the start line. I had read the schedule wrong and was an hour late! Only ten minutes to warm up. I was in a panic and quickly grabbed my bike and headed out to take a short spin. As I was frantically trying to exit the parking lot, Matt came riding up to me.

"Hey, what's up?" he said.

"I don't have time to talk now. I read the schedule wrong and I'm an hour late. I barely have time to warm up," I said hurriedly.

"It's okay," Matt said in a calm voice. "You've got a couple of minutes...come on and I'll ride with you."

He was so kind and laid back I couldn't help but calm down from my frenzied state.

After the race, I was back at my car packing up to drive on to the next location. Since every event was in a different town and the races were moving further outside of Milwaukee, I had to get to the next town and find a hotel.

Just then, Matt came up to me and said, "Hey, I'm headed to Madison to pick up a couple of friends who are flying in for the races and then we're going to stay at my brother's place for the night. He's out of town and his condo has a pool. Wanna come? It's a free place to crash."

Hmmmm, I thought. Free is good, but is this guy an axe murderer or rapist? My dad always taught me not to put myself in dangerous situations, but I did some quick analyzing of this guy, who was five-foot-six to my five-ten frame, and thought, I can

take him. Oh yeah, and you only live once. After all, this summer
is about adventure.

"Sure, I'll come," I finally said.

"Okay, I'm in that car over there. Just follow me. Here's my
cell phone number in case we get separated."

The whole time I was driving I was thinking, *I can't believe
I am going to follow this totally random guy to an unfamiliar city
and spend the night with him. Weird.*

When we got to his brother's house, we decided to take a
quick dip in the pool before Matt's friends arrived. As we played
in the water, we flirted and got to know each other. He was an
engineer from Philadelphia, just a year older than I was, and
seemed perfectly normal. And he had the cutest giggle. Not girly,
just a funny, happy laugh. I liked him instantly.

That night, we all went out to dinner—Matt, Steve, Eric
and me. It was just like hanging out with my group of racing
friends at home. We talked about bikes, bike racing, more bikes
and more bike racing. And the next day, we headed off to the next
event.

I spent the rest of the series with those guys. We drove to
races at the Oneida Indian Reservation and in Green Bay, and
each day after the race, we'd pack up and find a hotel in the next
race location. Matt gave up his car to Steve and Eric and he would
drive with me as we caravanned. It gave us a lot of quality time
to get to know each other and we fell fast. It wasn't until Paul, my
friend and training partner from home, came from Denver to join
us that things were cemented with Matt. We got to our next hotel

and there were three of us sharing one room. I was going to have to share a bed either with Paul or Matt. I was thinking it would be safer to sleep in Paul's bed, but he said, "I've been traveling all day, so I want my own bed."

That took care of that. And as we lay in the darkness of that hotel room, Matt and I kissed for the first time.

Chapter 3

After the accident, there was always someone with me in my hospital room. Matt and Andy took the overnight shifts and Mom was usually there during the day. And of course, there were the others—a constant flow of relatives and close friends.

I was worried about my family having to live at the hospital, but Mom said cheerily, "We've taken over the waiting room and let me tell you, it seems like a slumber party in there." They had brought pillows and blankets from home and a fellow racer, Derrick, had been supplying my family with pastries and juice in the morning and pasta and wine at night. They seemed entertained, so I tried not to think about it, but it was strange to have so much of people's time and attention showered on me.

News of my accident spread quickly through the cycling community. Between my stepbrother, Jeff, who was also a racer, and my training partner, Paul, the news got out quickly. Andy and my mom spent hours on the phone calling my other friends and telling them the news. People showed up at the hospital one after another after another, and cards, candy and stuffed animals were taking over my room. The flowers weren't allowed to stay in the ICU, but every time I got another bouquet, my mom would bring it in for me to at least see.

I tried desperately to be awake and coherent for my friends, but the truth was, I was on a morphine drip and in so much pain that all I wanted to do was be knocked out.

My nurse, Debbie, was very good about keeping the traffic at a somewhat manageable level. She would see me starting to nod off when I had visitors and promptly chase them out of my room. I always felt reassured when she was around. She was efficient and had a way of getting things done while still letting you know that she cared. I knew I was in good hands with her. Since I had never in my life spent a night in a hospital, I got attached to the people who took the best care of me, and in the beginning, Debbie was the only person I trusted. I would practically cry when her shift ended in the evening.

On Tuesday, when she came into my room, she told me that my surgery had finally been scheduled and would take place at 6 p.m. that evening.

"Tonight? But you won't be here then!" I panicked. *How am I going to get through this without her*? She seemed to know what I needed even before I did. Tears welled up in my eyes. I tried not to cry. I really did, but I could feel one tear sliding slowly down my cheek.

"Don't you worry about that," she reassured me as she patted my arm. "I will be here first thing in the morning when you're waking up."

Andy, sitting in the corner of the room said to Debbie, "Have I told you lately how wonderful you are?"

"Every time you see me." She gave Andy a quick smile and then left the room.

The rest of the day was spent waiting for the surgery, and as each of my family members flitted in and out of the room, I began to get nervous.

Sam, who was now acting as my primary liaison with the doctors, came in and explained the surgery. "We won't truly know the extent of the damage until they operate," he said as he spelled out all the gory details of what would come.

As he explained the procedure, my mind wandered. *What would they find? Perhaps things weren't as bad as they thought. Maybe my spinal cord was just bruised. Maybe...*

Sam brought me out of my thoughts. "They've given us a waiver for you to sign to approve the surgery." Andy, who was standing next to him, handed me the piece of paper and a pen. I took the pen in my right hand, but I couldn't grip it. My hand wasn't working. I was telling it what to do, but it wasn't listening. Finally, I took the pen in my left hand and wrote my name in chicken scratch.

That night, they finally rolled me into pre-op. I met with the anesthesiologist briefly so he could tell me how he was going to put me out. The nurse put a surgical cap over my hair and rolled me into the operating room. The anesthesiologist took out a syringe and connected it to my IV. One push of the medication and I started to feel woozy. And then...nothing.

* * *

When I finally woke up, I felt like a chipmunk. My face felt huge and I was staring out of slits where my eyes should have been. Everything was blurry and I felt disoriented. Andy and Greg were the first family members I remember talking to. Greg looked at me with this stare that seemed like terror covered up with a fake smile. Since I had been on my stomach with my head in a cradle for the six-hour surgery, my face was puffy and discolored. Apparently, I didn't look like myself. I looked like the Stay-Puft Marshmallow Man. Andy leaned over to kiss me and I could smell mint on his breath. "Hey, can I have a Tic-Tac," I asked before promptly falling back asleep.

We would laugh about my post-surgery state later. "Sam and Dad warned us that your face would be swollen," Greg said, "but I didn't think you'd look *that* funky."

Leave it to Greg to make me laugh in the midst of a serious time. It was just like old times when he'd try to make me giggle in church so I'd get in trouble.

Later, when Sam came into the room I knew I would get the whole story, like it or not. At first, I couldn't tell anything from his face. He wore his usual guarded look. His ice-blue eyes hid quietly behind those oversized glasses. He wasn't stoic like Dad, but he wasn't super emotional. He was level-headed. In this moment, he was all business.

"Well?" I asked. "Am I going to walk again?" No need to pussy-foot around. I wanted to know. I *needed* to know.

"The surgery went very well," Sam said, ignoring my question. "They put in two rods to stabilize your spinal column."

"And?" I was getting impatient. "What about my spinal cord?"

"It was worse than we thought," he said meekly, his eyes softening as his doctor "mask" came down and his emotions took over. "It's not severed, but it is bent in such a fashion that it has paralyzed you."

"Will I walk again?"

"Only time will tell, Trish. We're just going to have to wait and see."

"But there's a chance, right?"

"There's a chance, Trish," he said releasing a long breath.

That was all I needed to hear. There was still a glimmer of hope. *I would walk again, I just knew it.* I vowed I would walk out of the hospital.

Walking was for the long term, but in the short term I was ready to eat! It was now Wednesday morning and I hadn't eaten since lunchtime on Sunday. The doctor put me on a regular diet so I ordered a cheeseburger, fries and a big glass of lemonade. I snarfed almost all of it down and realized it wasn't going to stay there. "I'm gonna throw up!" Debbie came running in with an emesis basin.

"I...don't...feel...good," I stated the obvious.

As it turns out, due to the trauma my body sustained in the accident and the anesthesia from the surgery, my digestive system was a little slowed down. Actually, it was slowed to a stop. No one knew the extent to which I was backed up, but we quickly realized that I shouldn't have eaten a full meal because it wasn't going to go anywhere. It sat in my stomach like a brick and made me sick. In the following days, Debbie would try every laxative in the book to try to get me to have a bowel movement and some relief. It became a big joke amongst those closest to me. Greg would enter my room every day and say, "So Trish, did you poop yet?" Always the comedian, that guy. But he did his part by bringing me green tea and wheat grass shots.

I was getting worse and not better. My stomach was distended and I looked like I was pregnant. I was continuing to throw up and felt constantly nauseated. Debbie had to take a stand. "Trish, we can't have you like this anymore. I am going to have to put in something called an NG tube." I found out later that NG stands for "nasogastric" and it's a tube that they put up through your nose, down past your throat and into your stomach. Then they suck what's in your stomach right out. It's used for people who have intestinal obstructions or for cases like me where things just aren't moving. It didn't sound good, but who was I to doubt Debbie, she hadn't ever done me wrong. Until now. When she got the tube put in, it was absolutely the worst feeling *ever*. It felt like I had a Q-tip up my nose and a pencil in my throat. It hurt to swallow, talk and even just sit there. My eyes welled up with tears and I had a meltdown. Debbie watched patiently as I freaked out, threatened and whimpered, "Please. *Please* take it out."

"You have to have it, at least for a little while," she said sympathetically.

"I can't. I *can't* do this."

"You have to," she said, and walked out the door.

When she came in later, she could tell that I was still uncomfortable and completely unhappy. "Okay," she said. "Do three more hours and I'll take it out before my shift ends. I won't be here tomorrow, so I don't want to leave it in there if you're doing that badly."

Wait! What? Who said you could take the day off? Now I had a new reason to cry. A day without Debbie? As far as I was concerned, there *was* no other nurse who could take care of me. Another meltdown. Before she left that evening she came in and said, "Alright, I picked up an extra shift tomorrow. I'll see you in the morning."

Chapter 4

Debbie finally had to take a day off. My friends continued to pour in. The morphine continued to drip. And there was another reality I had to face. Andy had called Dave, who was in California, on a military training trip. It was next to impossible for Andy to figure out how to get in touch with him and then Dave had to get permission from his sergeant to come home. That Army stuff is serious. In fact, he hadn't been allowed to make any calls home since he left a week earlier. But he convinced his sergeant that our relationship was serious enough that he needed to return home. The only thing was that he didn't know anything about my whirlwind romance with Matt or that Matt was visiting Colorado—or for that matter, that Matt was at the hospital with me.

You know, a good mother will teach you to wear clean

underwear because, "you never know when you'll have an
accident and have to go to the hospital. You want to have clean
underwear on, don't you?" she would say. But I never once heard
my mom say, "Never have two boyfriends at once because you
might have an accident and you don't want both of them to show
up at the hospital, do you?" Oh, how I wish she had said that.

When I left Matt in Wisconsin after Superweek, I
headed off to Indiana to race in the Masters Nationals Cycling
Championships. I had to practically rip myself out of Matt's arms
to get in the car to drive away, but my plan after Indiana was
to go to a stage race in Pennsylvania called the Tour de 'Toona.
As luck would have it, Matt was from Pennsylvania and he was
going to be at that race also. So, we kissed and said goodbye
knowing we only had to make it another five days before we saw
each other again.

As I was driving from Wisconsin to Indiana, Dave called my
cell phone and said, "I want to see you. I'm coming to Masters."
Oh my.

He jumped in the car and by the next morning we were in
my hotel room together. *This is awkward.* But I couldn't break
up with him. He had driven sixteen hours just to see me for a
day and a half. Of course, he did a couple of races too, but he was
there for me. And my mind and my heart were already on the
way to Pennsylvania. Fortunately, he didn't stay the whole time
I was there and I figured that I would sort it all out when I got
home. But in the meantime, I was an independent woman on an
adventure.

I was jumping out of my skin when I saw Matt again in Pennsylvania. Instead of staying with my racing teammates, I chose to stay at his hotel with him. We raced during the day and had a date night every evening. It was like fantasyland. I forgot that I had another life back home. I was living the dream, riding my bike and hanging out with a cute guy. But of course, all good things come to an end. Our last night together was my birthday, August sixth. Matt took me out to the nicest restaurant in town, Red Lobster, for dinner. We were smitten and kept going over and over the details of the summer. It was perfect. Matt said, "We have to do this all again next summer. It'll be just like this year."

In the back of my head, I knew there could never be another summer so perfect, but I wasn't sure where those doubts were coming from. *It'll never be the same*, I thought.

The next morning I said goodbye, jumped in the car and headed home. Somewhere in the cornfields of Illinois, my phone rang and I was offered a new job within my local school district placing high school kids in internships. Slowly, my real life started to come back to me. *Oh yeah, I have a job and a non-fantasy life and Dave awaiting me at home.* Matt and I stayed in touch, talking and emailing a lot, but after being home a couple of weeks, I settled back into the real world and decided that my life was in Colorado. And since that was where Dave was too, I was going to try to make it work.

But Matt and I had previously made plans to see each other again, once in San Diego where he would be for work over Labor Day weekend, and a second time when he planned to come to

Colorado for a wine festival and bike tour. I decided to end our relationship in San Diego. That weekend was full of fighting and hurt feelings. It didn't go as smoothly as planned, but I let Matt know that I had to give Dave a chance. He was in my life first and he actually lived in the same state as me. Besides that, Matt and I were beyond the honeymoon period and I was beginning to find things about him that bugged me—he could be a know-it-all at times and somewhat closed-minded. I don't know why we decided it was still a good idea for him to visit for the wine festival, but we did. The day before Matt arrived, I said goodbye to Dave as he headed to California. At that point, I wasn't into him and I wasn't into Matt either. But I went through with my weekend plans and at the end of the weekend, I ended up here—in the hospital.

* * *

When Dave walked in, I could see he was crushed. His eyes were puffy and red and his face had that scrunched up look like he was about to cry. He had told me before he left that I was "the one." And now, here he stared at his "future wife" lying in bed, unable to move or do anything for herself. There was explaining to do about the ride, the accident, Matt, where we were to go from here. Dave took the accident so personally, like it happened to *him*. That made me fume because he could walk out of the room at any time and never come back. I didn't have that luxury. He sat in the waiting room and cried and threw fits and made my family crazy. He and Matt became competitive for my time and attention, and finally, both had to be reined in and put in their places by my brothers. This wasn't a time to try to win over a girl.

Breaking up all the craziness was Nurse Barb. We were the same age and when she came into my room to check on me for the first time she said, "All I want to know is how you know all these guys who keep coming in to visit!" I just laughed and filled her in on the Matt and Dave saga and my days of bike racing. There are probably five males to every female who races, so it's no wonder that most of my friends were guys.

"Well, I either need to start racing or hang out with you when you get out of the hospital," she said. I laughed at her comment, but realized for the first time that my life was going to be different when I got out of the hospital. *Will I ever race again? Will there still be guys who are interested in me if I'm in a wheelchair? What will my life be like?* Every night when I was alone in my hospital bed I would think and wonder and worry. I wanted so desperately to be confident that I would go back to my normal life, but when the lights would go out and the visitors left my room, I was devoured by anxiety.

Greg came into the room while Barb and I were talking. "It's so stuffy in here," he said. "This place sucks."

"You know, we could take you in your bed down the elevator and outside so you could get some fresh air," Barb said.

"Yeah! Let's do it" I stirred with excitement.

Barb took one end of the bed and Greg took the other and they pushed me right out of the ICU. All the other nurses just looked as we passed, probably wondering what we were up to.

When we got outside, I took my first breath of fresh air in a week. It felt good to be out of my hospital room, but it was a cruel reminder of what I was missing. The world was going on without me. And even worse, I didn't know to what extent I'd ever be able to participate again. Looking up at the brilliant blue sky, I missed my usual daily activities and riding my bike.

In the ICU, the nights continued to be a struggle. When the visitors were gone and the lights went out, the pain seemed to get worse. Dreams took over my consciousness. Dark dreams. A monster in the corner. Spiders crawling out of the sink. Ants marching across the ceiling. *I've got to get away. Move legs, move!* My legs wouldn't move even in my dream. *It must be a dream. A nightmare.*

The morphine was causing serious hallucinations and I was scared to drift off to sleep. Matt continued to stay with me at night, but I was getting more and more restless. Matt's dancing eyes had turned to pity and I was sick of him standing over me looking down at me that way. He had these big I'm-feeling-sorry-for-you puppy dog eyes and was continually touching and stroking me. I felt like I was in a petting zoo. And then things came to a head. We had *the talk.* I told him I couldn't be in a relationship with him. I was feeling claustrophobic. My family was getting far too involved in my personal life and in my medical situation, Dave and Matt were smothering me, and it was driving me crazy to lie in a bed all day. I had had enough and his relationship talk was the end of what I could handle. I knew he was hurting and that he still saw hope for us, but I wasn't in a place where I

could give him what he wanted. He told me I was selfish. My eyes
popped out of my head. I said as quietly and sternly as I could,
so no one else would hear, "You have no fucking idea what it is
like to lie here knowing you will never walk or ride a bike again. I
can't believe you're worried about a relationship when my life has
completely changed and will never be the same again."

The next time I saw Andy, I told him that it was time to
send Matt home. I couldn't deal with it any longer. Andy and
Matt had become good friends through all they had been dealt
in those first ten days, so I knew that Andy was the best person
to talk to Matt. No one could say, "Go home now" in a nicer way
than Andy. He's classy and tactful. And like that, Matt was gone.

Shortly after he left, I was moved out of the ICU to a
regular floor. No more Nurse Debbie or Barb. In fact, on the
regular floor, I felt like I barely got any attention and the initial
rush of visitors dropped off. My family started working on the
next step, which was rehab. They were looking at Craig Hospital
in Englewood, Colorado, but it was taking some hoop jumping
and dealing with red tape. The hospital therapists started to
come around to get me moving and help me sit up in a regular
sitting position rather than in a hospital bed that lifts to a sitting
position. The whole process was overwhelming to me because I
was still in so much pain. I had been lying in bed for so long that
I felt dizzy when I had to sit straight up. Each time, it took three
people to lift me up. I still had on a full back brace as well as a
neck collar and I had no idea how to assist them with getting
myself in position. Basically, they would play spin the bottle with

my body. I'd start out lying in the bed horizontally, then they would spin me half a turn so my head was off one side of the bed supported by one therapist and my feet would be off the other side, supported by another therapist, and then the third would grab my arms and support my shoulders and push me so I was sitting straight up on the side of the bed. Once I was sitting, the pain shot through my body, my head got woozy and I felt awful. I couldn't really feel my butt, so it was hard to get a feel inside my body for what was going on. I wondered how I was going to deal with this discomfort. *Is this really what it's going to be like everyday for the rest of my life?*

Finally, we got word that the move to Craig was going to happen, which was good because I was ready to move on. Andy started talking about how I would go to rehab and they would teach me more things beyond sitting up and then they would fit me for my wheelchair. When he said that, I flew off the handle. I looked him straight in the eye and said, "I am *not* going to go home in a wheelchair. I am going to walk out of that hospital and get back to *my* life." I pointed at my legs and said, *"This* is *not* my life!"

Although in my mind and my heart I knew that things had changed and this injury was permanent, I hated hearing it out loud or from other people. If they would just stop saying it, maybe it would end up not being true.

The day before I was scheduled to leave, I had breakfast just like the other mornings, but immediately afterward I started throwing up. Then I threw up again. And again. When the doctor came in, I already knew what she was going to say. I couldn't go to Craig until I was stable and somewhat healthy. She ordered more tests, blood draws. Troubleshooting. And I never really got an answer as to what they thought was wrong, but the next thing I knew, I was going into surgery again, this time to remove my gall bladder. Not again. The doctor. The anesthesiologist. The medicine. Drifting off to sleep...

When I awoke, I had the worst pain in my shoulder. Funny, but I didn't think my gall bladder was in my shoulder, but what I have learned since then is that *that* is where my body refers pain. Often after a surgery I find that I get awful shoulder pain. If I can't feel the incision in my abdomen, there's a good chance I'll feel it in my shoulder.

The good part about going in for surgery was that afterward, they put me back in the SICU. I was back to Debbie and the crew I knew and trusted and who came immediately after I pushed the call light. This time, during the overnights I had a new nurse, Pam. When she came to the door of my room, she looked directly at me; her head was cocked to the side with a look of true care and concern. She would sit on my bed listening to my complaints and my worries. She seemed to understand exactly what I was feeling.

Since I hadn't been able to take a shower or wash my hair or anything since my sweaty bike ride almost two weeks earlier, she said, "I think it's time for some pampering. I have some good-smelling soaps and lotions at home and I'll bring them in for you tomorrow night and we'll have spa time." The next night at about

10 p.m., when all the other patients were asleep and Pam could concentrate her energy on me, she came into my room and set up a basin and washcloths and started washing my hair. She kept the lights out, and in the dark it felt so good to unwind and have the warm water run over my scalp. She used one of my favorite Bath & Body Works scents. She made me feel relaxed and talked to me about my injury. She told me positive stories and assured me that things would be fine if I let them. It was just what I needed to hear.

After another week or so, the time when I would be transferred to Craig finally arrived. Debbie was there on my last day, which I was glad about. "I have doctor's orders here that you have to be off all of your pain medications before you're transported to Craig," she said. So that morning I didn't get any of my pills and she removed my Fentanyl patch, which gave me a constant stream of medication and was the number one reliever of the constant soreness and aches that still traveled through my back and scapula. At the time, I didn't realize that my body had come to depend on the painkillers for its daily fix.

As she walked out of the room and I lay there with my mother next to me, my brain began to rev up and kick into reality mode. *Wait a minute. I am leaving the hospital. I am leaving the place where they put you back together again and make you well, but...something is wrong. I am NOT well. I am never going to be well again. I can't walk! I can't move on my own. Oh my god, I am helpless. A fire, or gunman, or heaven forbid, Godzilla, could storm my room and there would not be one thing I could do to get*

*away, to defend myself. What's going to happen to me? I have not
gotten any better since I have been lying here on my back. I am not
well. Oh shit! Those medical miracle workers couldn't save me.*
The panic grew in me like a balloon until I burst out into a crying,
screaming tantrum. I yelled at my mother who was sitting not
two feet from my bed. "They are taking me away from here and
I'm not even well! They didn't fix anything. I can't move my legs. I
can't walk!"

Debbie came back later, followed by a team of paramedics
and a stretcher. Through tears I said my goodbye to Debbie.
She touched me lightly on my arm and wished me well. With
one paramedic at my head and one at my feet, they lifted me
by the sheet of my bed onto the gurney to roll me out to the
ambulance. My mother followed, holding my few belongings that
I had acquired at the hospital and wanted with me at Craig, and
we headed outside into the fresh air. Any other time it would
have been a day to embrace, with a turquoise blue sky, mild
temperatures and the crispness of fall. Instead, I felt weighed
down with grief and pain, as I was loaded into the back of the
ambulance.

I could see the hurt in my mom's eyes, but I didn't care. I
had my own issues to deal with and I was mad as hell that there
was no change, no difference in my life, but the hospital was just
going to shove me off and say, "Have a nice life."

The paramedics loaded me in the back of the ambulance
and shut the door. The engine revved up and off we went on the
ten-mile drive to Craig.

When I arrived at Craig, I was immediately taken to the third floor on the west side. That's where they put most of the new admits and sicker patients. You have to stay there until you are ready to really dive into rehab and get ready to go home. I was only three and a half weeks out from my injury and I had a long way to go.

A new nurse greeted me, but her name wasn't hard to remember—Debbie. I could only hope she'd be as good of a nurse as Debbie at St. Anthony. The new Debbie helped the transporters transfer me into my bed, and as they left, she introduced herself to me and said that my doctor would be in shortly. And with those few words, she was gone. My mom, Andy and I looked at each other a little puzzled, as we were used to the undivided attention that we received in the ICU.

As I lay in the bed with the side railings up, I felt like a baby in a crib. My mom and Andy stood on either side of me. I hadn't been lying there long before I started to feel agitated. My skin began to feel like it was crawling and I felt like an alien was going to come breaking out of my chest at any moment. I went back and forth between sweating and freezing and I grew increasingly restless. I started to panic and was moaning and groaning and wiggling any part of me that I could get to move.

"What is going on, Trish?" Andy asked.

"I don't know," I said in a frightened voice. "I just feel weird. I feel like I need to move my legs or walk or something and nothing will move. I have this horrible tingling in my body and it's making me feel stressed and shaky all over." When I started to totally freak out, my mom and Andy began to get worried.

"What do you think is wrong with her?" my mom asked Andy.

I don't know who finally figured it out, but collectively, we realized what was happening. I was going through withdrawal. All of my painkillers that I had been on for over three weeks had been quit cold turkey that morning and my body was rebelling.

Andy ran to get Debbie, but she said she couldn't do anything. Only the doctor could order the proper medications and she was still busy in meetings and seeing other patients.

"Can you tell her this is sort of an emergency?" Andy asked.

"I'll see what I can do," Debbie said.

It was so uncomfortable. *Please just kill me and get this over with.* In my mind, I began rating the torture of the last three weeks. This was definitely bad. The NG tube was worse, but this was second worst. The hallucinations were awful, but so was the pain. *Wow, this is making getting hit by a car the easiest thing I've done lately.*

My mom and Andy had me start counting, telling stories, saying the alphabet—anything to get my mind off of the withdrawals. They held both of my hands at once and got me a cool cloth for my forehead while I lay there whimpering and trying to move any part of my body that I could. Finally four hours after I arrived, Dr. Lanig walked in the room. She was an African-American woman, looked very self-assured, gorgeous and was dressed impeccably. She was calm, but I was not. My mom, Andy and I pleaded all at once. Drugs. We need drugs in this room. She quickly got to work ordering something to calm the effects of the withdrawal symptoms and a new regimen of painkillers. It didn't take long for the Ativan to kick in and I slipped into a happy restful state. I was out for the count.

The next day, it was down to business. Dr. Lanig came to see me first thing in the morning. We went through the accident and my medical history, which was quickly turning into a book of information, tests, and diagnoses. "So, you have a T-4 spinal cord injury, which means you are paralyzed at mid-chest level. In the accident, you broke your scapula and two ribs?"

"Yes," I concurred.

"Looks like a C-6 fracture and a brachial plexus injury." The brachial plexus is a collection of nerves normally protected by the scapula and shoulder bone and would account for the reason that my right hand hadn't worked when I tried to sign the surgery release form at St. Anthony.

"You've still got a neck brace on, but they discontinued your back brace. You're on your way to getting better, but we still have one major problem: your skin."

She was referring to the fact that I had a bedsore on my tailbone. It began during the long hours that I was on the backboard after the accident, and since there is no fat on that area of my butt, it wore a sore pretty easily. Then, during the time I was in St. Anthony, the pressure of lying in bed made the sore get worse instead of better. By the time I arrived at Craig, the sore was the size of a quarter and down to the bone. This is an extremely dangerous prospect as it's a breeding ground for bacteria and infection. In the old days, people with spinal cord injuries often died because of pressure sores. They are not to be taken lightly.

"We're going to try to manage it first and see if we can get it to heal, but if we can't you're looking at another surgery," she told me. "In the meantime, you won't be able to do much in terms of rehab, but I'll have your physical therapist see you each day to work on upper body strength and range of motion with you. Any questions?"

At that point, I didn't even know what to ask. I had no idea what rehab was going to consist of or what to even think. I just rolled with the punches.

The next day, Stacey, my physical therapist, started coming to visit me. She was my age with long, straight, chocolate-brown hair. She was a triathlete and in exceptional shape. I enjoyed the fact that she understood my obsession with bikes and racing, but it was also depressing knowing that she could walk out my door and head to her lunchtime workout. I quickly found out that was going to be the hardest part of my injury—knowing that there were certain things I *loved* that I would never do again. But it was nice to have someone to talk to that I had a lot in common with and I looked forward to her visit every day. Plus, she always gave me shoulder massages, which felt good because I had been cooped up, lying in a bed for days.

My skin sore stayed at the forefront in my beginning days at Craig and everyone who walked into the room wanted to look at my butt. I still wasn't used to the fact that your modesty goes right out the window when you're in the hospital, and I got agitated every time. It didn't matter if it was a nurse, Dr. Lanig, a therapist, an infectious disease doc, or skin doc—I was just plain tired of showing off my hindquarters. But finally, something had to be done and Dr. Lanig made the decision. This sore wasn't going to heal and I couldn't stay in the hospital forever waiting for it to do so. I was going to have to have what is called "flap" surgery. The surgeon cuts in a half-moon shape around your butt and then stretches the healthy skin over the wound. Then, you get massive IV antibiotics to kill any bacteria and infection, and you have to lie flat for six weeks so it can heal. And they're not kidding when they say lie flat. There is no sitting up…ever. Not to brush your teeth, look out the window or to eat—which, by the way, I hadn't done successfully since the cheeseburger back at St. Anthony. On November 2, I was admitted for surgery. And when I came out, I had fifty-six staples in my backside.

Now that it was taken care of, my job was to lie around and heal.

"You're on your way to recovery now," Dr. Lanig told me. "Now we just have to get you through six weeks of lying flat. You also need nutrition. You haven't kept any food down for weeks and without the necessary protein your skin won't heal. I'm going to order T-P-N for you."

"T-P what?"

TPN stands for Total Parenteral Nutrition, which is an IV liquid that basically provides all of your daily nutritional requirements. They inserted a central line IV into my chest where the TPN would continuously flow. Since eating only caused me to throw up, I didn't mind getting my food through the IV. I was tired of throwing up five times a day. I was beginning to forget about what it was like to eat real food and enjoy it anyway. And I had lost over twenty pounds, so I knew she was right about the nutrition.

Since the accident, I had sat up only a handful of times and been in bed the remaining several weeks, and now I was about to begin six more weeks of flat time. To give you an idea of where it falls on the torture scale, it is directly between the NG tube and the withdrawals. Only those forms of torture lasted a short time and were quickly cured, but I had no idea how I was going to get through six weeks without sitting up. The nurses and techs would come in and turn me every couple of hours, so I was always facing one wall or the other, but that was my only scenery. After about day two, I started to freak out. I was uncontrollably agitated. Not only was I lying flat, I also didn't feel well and some days were just unbearable. I asked Dr. Lanig if she could just put me out so I could sleep for the next six weeks. Then I could wake up and be better. She didn't go for that idea.

I continued to have this uncontrollable feeling that I needed to stretch my legs or move them around, but I still couldn't move them, and I couldn't even have someone move or stretch them for me because that would risk tearing my new skin flap.

Lying in the dark stillness of the night, with just the ceiling to stare at for comfort, the only thoughts booming through my head were regrets. I wasn't thinking of moving forward or what

my new life would bring. I kept thinking back to what I didn't
do and what I could never do again. If only I would have had
more time. What would I have done differently? Nothing earth
shattering. The things that came to mind were actually so simple
they hardly seem like anything worth giving a second thought,
but they were there, seeping into the crevices of my brain and my
body, tormenting me with the questions "why?" and "what if?"
As I lay there, I thought, *I should have worn my skirts shorter to
show off my long and lean cyclist's legs. I should have spent more
time snowboarding, run another marathon or done extra back
flips. I should have bared my true self and not been so reserved
when I really wanted to speak up, sing out or just be heard, all the
while not worrying what everyone else thought of me. I shouldn't
have dropped out of my final bike race because I was tired that day
and unable to keep up with the group. I should have dug deeper.
Why didn't I do more hiking in the Colorado mountains? I haven't
traveled the world yet. Or looked down on the earth from a hot
air balloon.* "You don't know what you've got 'til it's gone." That
saying could not have been truer for me, but then even *that* made
me mad because the people who say it probably have never lost
anything as vital. They can only imagine what it's like to lose
something so great, but does that saying really make them live
their life any other way? Do they think twice? *No,* I think. *They
don't know.* But I've graduated from the school of loss and have
the diploma on my wall to prove it. I know what it's like. And
regret cuts deep. It cuts like a knife.

* * *

All that time I lay on my back, there was one thing and one thing only guaranteed to make me smile. His name was Derrick.

Derrick was a fellow cyclist who, prior to my accident, I barely even knew. We had had exactly four occasions on which we had spoken previously. One: even though we were both from Colorado, we met at a bike race in Florida in 1998. He was nice and quite funny, actually, but at the time I was more focused on his cute friend. Two: I ran into him at a cyclocross race which I went to *watch* because I had never raced 'cross before. But he kept bugging me and telling me I should jump in with the other girls in my category. Finally, he had chided me enough that I did in fact do my first 'cross race that day. I loved it! Three: the day I ran my bike into a parking garage. I had just put my bike on the top of my car to head to a bike race when I stopped for bagels and tried to pull into a parking garage to park. With the scrape of metal above my head, I quickly realized that I had made a grave mistake. But, I had to be at the race because my team was putting it on, so I put my bike inside the car and drove to the race. When I got there, I was in tears and ran into Derrick. He asked me what was wrong. I told him about the incident and he said, "Let me look at the frame. Maybe it could be fixed." So I took him over to my car and gave him a look.

"Ummm, you're right. That's pretty well fucked," he said, looking at the frame.

Thanks. Earlier, on the walk to my car I told him I had

planned to do a duathlon the next day, but now I was screwed because I had no bike.

"Yeah, you know Trish, a duathlon without a bike is really just a marathon," he said in his usual sarcastic tone.

"I appreciate your working hard to cheer me up," I said in a matching sarcastic tone. I could tell already there was some sort of vibe between us, but I could tell he was somehow unreachable.

I spent that whole day moping at the races and at one point while I was sitting on a corner watching the bikes blur by, he came up to me with a paper bag in his hand and said, "I got you something, Trish."

"What?"

"Mood enhancers," he said cheerfully.

"Huh?"

Just then he pulled out a six-pack of beer and opened a can and handed it to me. I just shook my head and smiled. He sat down on the curb and entertained me the rest of the afternoon.

And Four: as I was riding out to Lookout Mountain one day, I heard a car trailing behind and someone yelling at me. I didn't recognize the car or the voice, but it was making me very angry. *Just go around*, I kept thinking. But it kept following me and I was getting so pissed. Finally, I decided I was going to stop and give this stupid driver a piece of my mind. So I pulled over and stopped and the car stopped right next to me. "What the..." I started to yell and then I realized it was him. "Derrick, you know how annoying that is to have someone driving behind you like that when you're on your bike!"

"I know. I was trying to get your attention. What are you doing?"

"Duh...I'm riding."

We stopped and, in the middle of the street, had about a half-hour conversation. I was nervous and giddy like a schoolgirl, because not only did I think he was totally cute with his smiling brown eyes and a grin that stretched across his face, he was an awesome bike racer and I was wondering why he seemed to pay so much attention to me. Finally he said, "Follow me home, I'll get rid of my car and we'll go for a ride." It wasn't even a question, but if it were, he wouldn't have had to ask twice. The whole way to his place, I thought, *This is weird, but YEE-HA!* I did the happy dance in my head.

I followed him home and into the house. He ran into his bedroom, changed and came back into the living room to put on his shoes. I couldn't think of a thing to say. I felt like I was in middle school again with a big, fat crush. We headed out the door and hit the road.

He was so fun to ride with. He talked the whole time and made me laugh so hard I didn't even realize how hard I was working to keep up with him. He never tried to be macho and ride off in front of me like some of the other guys I rode with. He just stayed right there at my side. We rode to Lookout Mountain, up to the top and back down again. Then we rode around the city, to Washington Park and just *around*. It was like the bike ride that neither one of us wanted to end. Finally the sun set and the sky turned black. Neither one of us had lights on our bikes, so he rode home with me. In front of my house we said a very long goodbye.

"Do you want to come in? How about a glass of water? Or maybe some beer?" I offered to drive him home.

He smiled at me and said, "I had fun tonight." I smiled back and in one moment, he scurried off.

That was the last time we talked until my accident.

When Derrick heard word of my accident, he was one of the first people at the hospital. He constantly showed up with meals for my family and a bright smile and lots of jokes for me. When he'd visit I'd feel the weight of the world lift from my shoulders and a ray of hope return to me. He made me laugh so hard that when he left, I would be exhausted and sleep for hours. I'd be worn out and would need some serious down time to recover. At one point, my Mom suggested we keep Derrick's visits to a minimum because it took so much out of me. But I was living to see that smile, those happy brown eyes and his upbeat attitude.

I was touched to read the article that he submitted to our local racing newsletter about me. It read:

TRULY, A FALLEN COLORADO ANGEL

On Sunday, September 17th, one of Colorado's wonderful women's riders, Tricia Downing, was struck by an automobile head-on while riding her bicycle with her friend Matt down 32nd Avenue outside of Golden. Trish suffered not only a broken scapula and broken ribs, but also sustained major fractures in several of her vertebrae. The good news is that she was wearing a helmet and there were no closed head injuries. However, at this point the extent to which she will recover is still unknown. Although things are not as good as they might be, rest assured even despite her injuries, Trish is still brimming with the overwhelming positive attitude that makes her Trish.

Tricia Downing is an active Colorado racer who is not only competitive on the road and track, but also spent time racing on a tandem piloting blind cyclists at national events. As important as her contributions to Colorado cycling are her contributions to this world and making it a better place. To know Trish is to truly be blessed. Her radiant, ever-present smile coupled with her unbridled positive attitude emits healing powers. After a couple minutes talking to Trish, nothing ever seems quite so bad—she is an angel. For those who are friends with Trish, I share in your sorrow and will share in your praying. For those who are unfamiliar with her, please include her in your thoughts and prayers. I can assure you she not only deserves them, but also in a reversed situation, would undoubtedly include you in hers.

Derrick was my knight in shining armor. When I was moved to Craig, he started visiting even more. He would tell me how he wished he could pick me up and whisk me away to some exotic beach somewhere. We'd just sit together in our lounge chairs and drink cocktails. It sounded way better to me than lying on a bed in the hospital.

"How are we going to afford to move away to a beach?" I asked him.

"We'll just have to win the lottery," he answered easily.

From then on, he brought me lottery tickets on Wednesdays and Saturdays and we'd pay attention to the drawings to see if our dream was going to come true. If he'd come by when I was sleeping, I'd find the ticket taped to my bed somewhere. Sometimes he'd draw me cartoons and leave those for me. No matter what it was that he left, it would make me feel all warm and fuzzy inside that he cared so much.

One night, he was in visiting and we were all alone in my room. We talked about anything and everything. I could tell him truly how I felt because I knew he wouldn't feel sorry for me. He was empathetic. I could tell he was feeling my pain and doing everything he could to share the burden. I asked him why he didn't come into my house after our long ride that day at the beginning of the summer. "I knew that could only lead to trouble," he said to me and smiled.

I remembered one of my favorite quotes a classmate used in my high school yearbook: *The trouble with trouble is that it starts out as fun.* "I guess you could make up for it now," I said with raised eyebrows and a shrug of my shoulders.

"I guess so," he said, and leaned over to kiss me. In my mind I thought, *Was that for real?* Then he kissed me again. *Oh yeah.*

We looked each other in the eyes and both knew we had just started something. There was no going back. Our relationship just took one giant step forward.

When he left, I wanted to jump up and down and do somersaults...but I couldn't. It didn't matter, though, because a thousand butterflies danced in my stomach.

Chapter 5

I had a calendar hanging on the wall in my room and Andy would carefully check off the squares so I could see how, day-by-day, I was getting closer to the six-week mark. But it wasn't helping. I was mad, bitter and uncomfortable. I lashed out at people, including my mother. I have never yelled at her in my life, but one day she made mention of my less than stellar attitude, and on that very day, the criticism hit me like a sledgehammer.

"I'm tired of you and I'm tired of this!" I screamed at her. "You have no fucking idea how I feel! I wish I would have died in that accident and I wish you would just leave me alone!" I regretted those words the minute they came out of my mouth, because I knew they hurt my mother right down to the core. But that was how I was feeling and I was tired. Just plain worn out. Trying to be optimistic when your whole being is pulling you straight down the drain is exhausting. I was done.

Dr. Lanig ordered acupuncture to try and calm my nerves. She prescribed anti-anxiety drugs. She had me moved to the east side of the third floor, which is reserved for patients who are doing well, rehabbing and working toward discharge. My new room had large windows and a separate sitting room with a couch and a refrigerator. It was like my own apartment. Stacey continued to give me daily shoulder massages. Anything to get me through. My friend Paul brought me special glasses that you can wear when you're lying on your back. They have mirrors in them so that you can see something on the wall, or TV, as was the case, in front of you. That way, I could watch movies without having to sit up. Because the TPN was such complete nutrition, my nails were growing like they never had before, and Lisa brought in a manicurist to give me French manicures. One of my techs would braid my hair and the respiratory therapist would spend extra time in my room in the middle of the night just to talk to me when I couldn't sleep. Thanksgiving came and went and I got to eat a little turkey lying on my back, surrounded by my family. Everyone did his or her part to get me through.

At the end of November, it was finally time to start sitting up. Not so fast, though. You can't just sit up after skin surgery— especially not after you've been lying in bed for over two months. I began a "sitting program," which basically meant I could sit up a little at a time, until my skin was stretched and it was safe to sit the whole day. I began each sitting session by taking a pill to help raise my blood pressure about a half hour before I got out of bed. I had to have that because since I had been down so long, I would get dizzy spells when I sat up. Then the therapists would help me up and into a high back wheelchair. The first day, I got two sessions of fifteen minutes each. The next day, two sessions, thirty minutes each. And I worked my way up from there, until I could sit up almost the entire day. Then...it was time to move. I had already been at Craig almost two months and I had a lot of work to do. Since insurance wasn't going to pay for me to stay in there much longer, I had to get going.

Just because you're in a wheelchair doesn't mean those folks at Craig let you spend a lot of time "sitting on your butt." Every morning, the nursing tech is in your room waking you up at seven a.m. to get ready for a full day of classes. For me, they'd come in and give me my blood pressure pill and breakfast. Then it was time for a bed bath, and getting dressed. Boy, that felt good. It was so nice to finally wear real clothes, even if they were just sweat pants. I put on a bra and shoes for the first time since the accident—even got to comb my hair and look in the mirror. Oh the things you take for granted when you're not stuck lying flat in a hospital bed.

My days were full of classes, much like high school. I called it Life 101. First, there was physical therapy, then occupational therapy, wheelchair class, weightlifting and nursing education. Every morning, as soon as I got dressed I had to hurry through the hallway and to the rehab gym.

On my first day, Stacey met me at the door. She had this great big smile and always looked truly happy to see me. She motioned to an elevated mat in the middle of the room and said, "Let's go over there, Trish." I pushed my chair over until it was touching the mat. Stacey got in front of me and bent her legs, then gave me sort of a bear hug and transferred me from my chair to the mat. Then she laid me down and gently swung my legs around so that I was lying on my back with my whole body on the mat.

She sat next to me and said, "Okay, Trish—the first thing you have to learn to do is sit up. Then we'll get to work on your transfers so you can move from your chair to the bed, bath bench, couch and any other place you'll need to get to."

I looked at her with a puzzled expression. *Sit up, huh? What kind of remedial lesson is this? What kind of idiot does she think I am? This is like, the most basic movement ever. I've done this first thing in the morning every day of my life.* So I did what I had always done—flexed my abdominal muscles (so I thought) and let that signal travel from my brain to my body, which says, "Sit up." And as I engaged the proper channels and attempted to sit up, nothing happened. Not a muscle in my body moved. Suddenly, I was panic-stricken. Stacey explained to me that since my paralysis was from the mid-chest down, I no longer had the ability to recruit my core muscles to do something as simple as sitting up. In that very moment, my eyes bulged out of my head and for the first time, I began to realize just how serious my injury was. My cheeks felt flush and my eyes filled with tears.

Stacey could tell I was on the brink and she told me, "Trish don't worry. We do have a long way to go and you will get there.

Just be patient. You will still be able to do all the things you used to do, but you're going to have to learn new ways to do them."

That would end up being the statement that elevated my blood pressure and made me want to hit someone. More times than I could count during my time in rehab, able-bodied therapists at Craig would tell me that "you can still do all the same things you used to do..."

And all I would hear in my mind was "Blah, blah, blah, you're paralyzed and I'm not."

Of course that was my own bitterness coming out and it would take me years to realize that they were, in fact, quite accurate. But back then...I wasn't having it—even though at the end of that first session, she had taught me to roll over and press up with one hand, drive my elbow into the mat and then with one final push, arrive at a sitting position. I couldn't believe how much work it took just to sit up. It was like all the energy I had for the day. I couldn't imagine how I would ever get any further than just getting out of bed each day.

Getting out of bed was one of the next things I learned. Dr. Lanig had my hospital bed moved out of my room and a regular queen-sized bed moved in. That was how they got you ready to go home. The environment in the east side rooms was meant to duplicate as closely as possible that which you would experience at home.

After I learned to sit up, we worked on transfers—moving from one seat to the other. Then it was on to my room where I learned to transfer to my bed, the toilet seat and the shower chair. Stacey and I would practice as many transfers as we could each day. She would grab just under my knees and my job was to push up with my arms and pivot my butt toward whatever it was I was trying to transfer to. She gave me that little extra 'umph' that I needed because my arms were so weak from lying in bed for three months.

The transfers were going pretty well until one afternoon when I got the bright idea to do one by myself, in my hospital room with the door shut. I thought I would get out of my chair and chill for a while on the couch. But when I decided to get off the couch, I realized, in a state of alarm, I was stuck. The couch was too low, too squishy and I couldn't get the lift I needed to get back to my chair. I was nowhere near the call button. The nurses couldn't hear me yelling through the heavy door of my hospital room. I looked around for my cell phone, but it was way over on the night table by the bed. *What do I do?* I broke into a sob. *I can't believe this is my life! Why me?*

Finally, Paul came by and opened my door a crack. "Trish?" he said.

"Can you help me?" I whispered from the sitting room.

He opened the door and came in. I felt pathetic and helpless sitting there on the couch, looking up through my tears. He grabbed my knees like Stacey did and helped me off the couch. "I am *never* sitting on that couch again," I said.

Paul cracked a smile to lighten the mood and I couldn't help but give a half smile back. Still, I was more than a little pissed.

* * *

In the basement of Craig hospital, they have even more props to help you learn real life skills. There is a car and even airplane seats so that you can practice your transfers. Stacey took me through each of them many times, determined that I would be as independent as possible when I left the hospital.

One day during therapy, Ina, my occupational therapist, and I took a "walk" to the grocery store. It was the furthest I had pushed my wheelchair, but I needed the endurance work. We gathered the ingredients we needed to make a pizza and then headed back to the kitchen in the rehab gym at Craig. She helped me around the kitchen and we worked on things like opening the oven and refrigerator doors and cooking from the chair, which, for someone like me who doesn't cook anyway, was a little bit of a challenge. Reaching above you to do things on the counter or in the sink is difficult in a kitchen built for someone who is standing, but it's what you have to deal with when you go home. So we worked at it.

In wheelchair class, we learned how to do wheelies and open doors. In the nursing education class, we learned about things like skin care, sex and peeing. Skin care, I had that down. *Never* get a sore again. It's miserable. Sex? I skipped that class. I wasn't sure why that was offered anyway. I got hit by a car. I didn't forget how to have sex. Plus, I was also in a state of denial. I wasn't sure that I had much of a dating life ahead of me. Peeing? That was another story. That's not something you can avoid.

Since the moment I was admitted to the hospital, I had an indwelling catheter and a bag of pee constantly hanging off my bed, which the techs would come in and empty every few hours. It was such a non-issue that I never gave a thought to how I would actually carry out the act of peeing when the catheter was removed. It was in my new queen-sized bed that I finally found out. One day, Nurse Vicky came into my room and said it was time to learn about intermittent catheterization. Intermittent what? In order to be able to pee, I had to insert a catheter into my urethra and pee into some sort of container, and Vicky was the lucky nurse who had the job to teach me how to do this delicate procedure. She had me get on the bed, lie back and showed me where to insert this catheter, which looked like a silicone version of a swizzle stick. It's akin to inserting a tampon except the hole you are aiming for is like the size of the "O" character on a keyboard and *not* easy to find. It took probably half an hour for me to locate it just once. By the time I got it, I was steaming with frustration, humiliation and just plain despair. *This is what I am going to have to do every time I want to empty my bladder from now on?* I even asked Vicky through tears, "Do I really have to do this every time?" Well, there were other options, she told me....I could keep the indwelling catheter and bag, or have a supra pubic catheter surgically put in me so there would always be a tube coming out of me right at the pubic hairline, but I would still have the bag that I would have to empty regularly. As she talked to me, tears rolled down my face. She was so sympathetic to the situation and I could tell that it hurt her to have to give me this news. She sat on my bed and just hugged me and told me that over time, it would get easier. "That's what everyone keeps telling me about everything. It's not going to get better! This is my life now and I don't want it. This is not my fault. I didn't ask for this! It's all somebody else's fault and I have to live with it." I couldn't talk anymore through the tears and the pain. Every time I thought about it, my heart sank and I got that nauseous feeling that comes from knowing things have gone dreadfully wrong.

At the hospital, you had to *cath* every six hours. The nurses would keep the schedule and track you down wherever you were and announce to you, "Time for IC," and then they would follow you back to your room, hand over the supplies and when you were done, check your output. If it were over 500cc, you would get a scolding because any more volume than that is not good for your bladder. Clearly, these ladies had never been out with me for a night of drinking in college. You know how beer makes you pee. I'm pretty sure I've peed a gallon at one time or another. I guess that's one of the reasons alcohol was not allowed in the hospital at Craig, but just to stir things up a bit, Derrick would sneak wine in for me on occasion and we'd drink it from the wax-covered Dixie cups that they had in the hospital.

A lot more happened in that bed than learning to pee. No sex, but it really was the only place to sit in the main part of the room, so there would often be times that I had four or five friends in bed with me. We'd all be lying intermingled together and watching TV, or sitting and drinking wine, but every time a nurse would knock on the door, everyone would bolt to an upright fashion, ditch the drinks and sit at attention when the nurse walked in. I felt like I was back in high school getting caught sneaking some of Dad's alcohol from the pantry.

As a result, I always seemed to be the talk of the nurses' station. Since I was a hometown girl and many of the Craig patients were from out-of-state, it seemed like I always had more of a constant stream of people in my room. I got more cards, presents and visitors than probably anyone else. And when Derrick would stay late into the night, one time until two a.m., I was a serious source of gossip. I found this out because when the morning crew came in the next day they'd say, "I heard you had a big night last night." Or, "Sounds like you had a late night visitor." Nothing ever "happened" in that bed, except maybe some making out. Some nights it was just a place to let go and cry. Even though Derrick was a clown most of the time, there were moments when he'd sober up his joking ways and listen to me talk about the emotional pain I was feeling. I remember one night lying in bed in his arms, just going on and on. "This isn't my fault! I hate it! I don't want to be like this." And he just listened and hugged me.

"I know, Trish," he consoled. "It's going to be okay, though."

"I can't do anything I like to do anymore."

"When you get out of the hospital, we'll find things that you can do. I promise."

"Well, what if nobody thinks I'm pretty anymore?"

"I think you're pretty. Still. Always. In fact, I think you're smokin' hot!"

It made me feel better to hear those words. It also made me believe he'd always be there for me.

Chapter 6

Since I was finally feeling better, my skin was healthy and I was mobile I got a visit from the recreational therapist. She bounced into my room one day and said, "Hi Trish. I'm Claire. I'm a recreational therapist and my job is to teach you the fun stuff. I hear you're an athlete?"

"Yeah, I used to be a cyclist," I said bitterly.

"You can still be a cyclist. You can still do all the same things you used to do, you know? You just have to learn new ways of doing them."

I rolled my eyes.

"Really, you can do the things you used to do. I can teach you. You came in here an athlete and I'm going to make sure you leave here an athlete. Tell me what kind of things you'd like to do."

All I could think about was riding a bike. I had finally found something that I loved to do and that I was getting better at every day. It was hard to believe I would never do it again.

I always liked riding bikes. After all, it was my main form of transportation for the first fifteen years of my life. Without my bike, there would have been no way to get to the pool and swim team practice, no riding with the neighbor kids to the playground or pedaling to Dairy Queen with my family on summer nights. But I didn't develop a passion for it until I did an internship for graduate school at the Olympic Training Center. I was finishing a Masters Degree in Physical Education and Sports Management at Eastern Illinois University when my professor asked me one day how I might like to do an internship at the OTC. My eyes nearly popped out of my head. "I would love that! In fact, it would be a dream come true," I exclaimed. She gave me the application and I filled it out immediately. During the summer of 1995, I was accepted and placed at USA Cycling, the national governing body for the sport of cycling in the United States. At the time I knew nothing about bike racing, but I loved sports and knew I could learn. As it happened, they were a little short staffed in the office so I was flown around the country as part of the communications team to cover road and track races for junior, master and elite racers. It was such an exciting sport. Speed, tactics, crashing. Amazing. My favorite was watching the track races at the velodrome. I couldn't believe those bikes didn't have any brakes and only one gear. *How do they ride on that steep bank...and go so fast? I have to try that!* All summer I watched these races and dreamed about getting on a track bike and giving it a go. My internship was soon over, but I never stopped thinking about someday getting on the track.

That fall, I got a job as communications director with USA Table Tennis and had the great opportunity to be the table tennis team press officer at the 1996 Olympic Games in Atlanta, Georgia. It was so fun to go to the various venues and see these conditioned athletes compete. It made me miss my athletic past and competition. Since my days as a high school gymnast and college diver, I had become a couch potato and hadn't had much to do with sports at all. But after my time at the OTC and the Olympics, I was motivated to find a way to get back into the loop.

When I returned home to Colorado Springs from the Games, my friend Michelle told me about a beginner women's clinic at the velodrome and asked if I wanted to go with her. I jumped at the opportunity and the next week, we went to learn how to ride fixed-gear bikes without brakes. It was a blast! I loved having the wind blowing by my cheeks as I rode down the embankment and around the turns. I felt so free. It was empowering, exciting and something so new to me. I adored it. But, I wasn't in very good shape for speed or endurance and several of the racers around the track told me that I needed to get out on the road to get some miles in my legs.

At the same time, I had changed jobs to work at USA Swimming and was forming a friendship with Larry, a co-worker of mine. I told him all about my new racing hobby and how I wanted to become an elite-level cyclist. Larry was a college

swimmer and since we were both the competitive type, we
constantly bantered about who was the better athlete. Then,
one day we resolved to settle the argument once and for all. We
decided to compete in a local sprint triathlon. Because we both
thought we were so great, we settled on one that was only about
a week and a half away. Larry had been spending his lunch hours
swimming, so he was pretty confident on that front. He didn't
even own a bike. I, on the other hand, hadn't been in the pool for
awhile, but had been doing a few of the weekly races at the track.
As for running, neither one of us had any business trying to go
further than down the block. Larry purchased a bike four days
before the race and we went through with our bet on who would
finish first in this triathlon—a 525-meter swim, 12-mile bike and
a 3-mile run. To say it was an ugly display of lack of fitness would
be an understatement. We both finished, stumbling across the
line, tongues hanging out and ready to collapse at any moment.
That race quickly put us in our places and neither one of us had
much to brag about afterward. But what it did do was inspire us
to start training and get in shape!

We began going to the Air Force Academy several nights
after work to ride a seventeen-mile loop. In the beginning, we
thought that was really something. It seemed like such a long ride
and we'd go home just plain beat. But after awhile, we started
building our strength and endurance, and we were able to go for
longer and longer rides. We also began to compete in running
races every weekend. Mostly 5Ks and 10Ks, but we also flew to
San Diego together to do a marathon. Eventually, Larry started

getting serious about triathlons and I decided to concentrate on my bike. I hired a coach to help me since I knew nothing about training or racing and he promised to help me take things up a notch. One day, my coach proposed something that would change my life. He called me and said, "Trish, I have a great opportunity for you. There is a training camp being held for athletes with disabilities at the Olympic Training Center and I know of a blind athlete who needs a tandem pilot to participate at the camp. He's relatively new to cycling like you are, and I think it would be great if you two could learn together. Plus, you will learn your bike handling skills twice as fast if you're forced to learn them on the tandem. I think it's a win-win situation."

Who was I to say no? I already worked at the OTC, so it's not like it would be going out of my way, and I was totally game to help out a fellow cyclist. I had never known anyone with a visual impairment before, so I knew I'd have a lot to learn, but I was up for the task.

The cyclist's name was Randy. Randy was a little bit older than I was, married and living in the Springs. He had heard about the camp and wanted to check it out. We had little in common, but he was nice enough and I was interested to see how this experience would go. As a tandem pilot, my job was to be the eyes of the operation and to steer. We both pedaled to the best of our abilities to power the bike. It was a true team effort. Randy had to pay attention to my voice commands and body motion and I had to keep him informed of everything going on. If we weren't in sync, we could easily crash and get hurt. We only spent about three and a half days together at that camp, but my skills increased exponentially. In addition, we learned about training, nutrition and all of the race opportunities available to us. It gave me a whole new excitement about bike racing to be a part of the clinic, and Randy became a regular training and racing partner for me.

The camp also included other athletes with disabilities, including wheelchair athletes. This was yet another experience for me because I hadn't known anyone with a spinal cord injury before, so I got an introduction to that, too. In fact, during a weight lifting session, I sat next to one of the wheelchair athletes and got up the nerve to ask him about his injury. He was injured crashing off a motorcycle. He told the story in such detail that I could see every motion as it happened. I pictured him lying on the ground, not being able to move. He told me then that as he lay there, he couldn't feel his legs. He said it felt just like his body was lying on the concrete and his legs were floating in the air. As I listened to his story that day, I had no idea that just two and a half short years into the future, I would know that exact feeling. I couldn't realize how that story would touch me but in the moment I hit the ground on that September day, it would come rushing back to me. That's exactly how I knew, at the scene of my accident, that I, too, was paralyzed.

That camp was also a blessing. As I watched these athletes go about their lives and their sports, I realized that a physical disability was not, in fact, the end of the world. It was not something that I had yet experienced, but these athletes didn't seem much different than me. They loved racing, had high hopes for themselves and lofty goals—just like my own cycling ambitions. The best thing to come from my experiences with these athletes was that when I was at Craig Hospital and Claire came into my room for the first time, I knew something about wheelchair sports. I knew there were opportunities out there for me. And even though I had a long way to go through some very difficult physical, mental and emotional adjustments, I had the knowledge and the experience to really help me hit the ground running (or rolling, you might say).

I told Claire that I wanted to try riding a handcycle. I had seen the wheelchair athletes ride them at camp and even tried one for about two minutes. "Maybe I could check out a racing chair, too," I added. Albert, the friend and wheelchair racer I had met during the Hood-to-Coast race prior to my injury, had used one of those when we competed together on our relay team.

"That all sounds good, Trish. I'll get clearance from Dr. Lanig and then you can come down to rec therapy and jump on a bike."

The next day, I was in the rec room with two therapists lifting me out of my chair and on to the handcycle. Paul had brought his bike to the hospital to ride with Claire and me. Claire got into another handcycle and said, "Are you ready to have fun, Trish? Let's go!"

We headed out of the hospital, on a sunny December day, exited the parking lot and headed north. Within moments, we found ourselves at the first stop sign. I stopped, and as Paul and

Claire looked both ways and then crossed, I continued to sit at the stop sign. It was my first time back on the road after being hit and I wasn't sure I could cross the street. "What's wrong, Trish?" Claire yelled across the street.

"Is it clear?" I asked.

"Yeah, come on across," she replied.

"Are you sure it's clear?" I asked.

"Yes, Trish, it's clear."

"Still?" I yelled.

"Yes, still. Come on!"

I was finally coaxed to ride across the street. We kept riding through the neighborhood until we found a good parking lot to ride around in circles so I could see how the handcycle worked. Claire got out of her handcycle and let Paul take it for a ride. The two of us had races through the parking lot, but I couldn't keep up with him. After almost three months of lying in bed, I had no endurance left and very little strength in my arms. In fact, my biceps were so thin, I could circle them with my middle finger and thumb. After only a half hour I was beat so we rode very slowly back to the hospital. Fortunately, having been a cyclist, I knew that even though I had no strength or endurance, those were things that could be built with enough time and effort.

At the same time I was learning to ride the handcycle, I was relearning to drive. The hospital owned several cars with hand controls, and part of rehab is learning to use those controls and then going for the driver's test. You have to have special provisions on your license to legally operate hand controls. When

I first got in the car, I had the same problem that I had had on the bike. I was scared to be around other cars and in traffic. I felt like I was a teenager learning to drive for the first time.

So many things were happening all at once. Life 101 was stuffing everything I had learned in the past thirty-one years, into a one-month session so I could get back out into the world and, with any luck, live as independent a life as I had prior to my injury. Christmas was just around the corner and instead of being happy and festive, I felt like I was cramming for finals. I had to learn everything I could and figure out where I was going to live and what I was going to do once I got out of the hospital.

In an effort to lighten the stress and to do something to cheer me up, one day my mother suggested that we go shopping. I was finally allowed to have a day pass out of the hospital, so she thought this would be a good opportunity to get out and unwind. "I'll go get the car and meet you at the drive-up entrance," Mom said to me. I put my heavy winter coat over my stylish sweats that were now my daily fashion wear, and took the elevator down to the first floor. As I passed through the sliding doors, I looked up at my mother's car. At the time, she drove a Ford Excursion, which is like the biggest car on the planet. When I was learning to transfer, I practiced on a small car, about the size of a Honda Accord, in the basement of Craig Hospital. The Excursion is many feet higher and not an easy transfer. Even to this day, I cannot get into a car that size all by myself. My mom came over to my chair as I placed it inside the crook between the open door and the seat, and I just looked up, feeling like an ant that was preparing to climb a fourteener. We tried every way to push, pull and shove me into that car, but between our collective lack of know-how and strength, we couldn't get me up to the passenger seat. To make things worse, my mom was afraid that if we had someone from the hospital help us, we'd have the same problem at the other end and not be able to get me back in the car after shopping. I wanted to be tough and act like it didn't matter, but it did. It was like another slap in the face. My mind was telling me, *See, here's one more thing you can't do. Your life is a joke. You can't do the simplest of things. Why don't you give up now?*

I didn't have a reply to my thoughts and just sat there and cried silently. I looked up at my mom and she had the same teary, sorrowful look on her face. "I'm so sorry, honey," she said. "I wish I could just make all of this go away, but I can't. I promise we'll figure it out, though."

I headed back to my room and spent the rest of the day sulking.

The highlight of this time was the fact that Claire kept showing up and encouraging me to learn new activities and go on trips with the rec therapy department. I went to the rodeo, and made Christmas presents for my family. There were movie nights and poker games. I started socializing with other patients and realized that while things were difficult, I was not alone. The people at Craig Hospital were turning into my family. I met a couple, Chris and Renee, who would become dear friends. Chris had had an accident almost exactly like I had, and on the same day. He, too, was riding home on his bike and was hit by a car. He sustained a T-4 spinal cord injury. He had a few additional injuries and was airlifted from Boulder, where the accident happened, to Denver for surgery and a stay in the ICU. September 17, 2000 was a bad day.

I remember when I was first hurt and in the ICU. I had received a stack of cards and in one of them, a fellow cycling competitor had written, "I am so glad you are okay. Knowing what happened to you, I am reminded of what a dangerous sport cycling can be sometimes. It makes me sad knowing what happened to you and Nicole, and on the same day." I looked up at my mom with a puzzled look and told her what the card said. My mother, who didn't even know exactly who she was talking about, but had learned the news from several of my friends, said, "Nicole Reinhart died on Sunday from injuries she sustained from a crash in a bike race." The news hit me like a ton of bricks, not only because I realized how my injuries could have been so much worse, but because I had actually met Nicole at a bike race earlier in the spring. I was struck by how kind and genuine she was. She was an elite cyclist, and to her, I should have been a nobody. But she was nothing short of gracious. A class act. That weekend, I admired her and her teammates, wishing that one day I could race alongside them. They say bad things happen in threes. September 17 definitely had its share of tragedy.

Chapter 7

Next on my rec therapy list was learning how to push the racing chair. This was a little more difficult than the handcycle because there is special equipment and a lot of technique to learn. A racing chair is a three-wheeled machine with a bucket seat and push rims that are on the wheels, similar to a regular chair. You use special gloves and there is a particular way to strike the rims to propel yourself forward. There are no gears like on the bike, so it's harder when you get to a hill because there is no way to make it easier as you go up. Claire showed me a short video to give me the gist of how to push the chair, and then we tried it at a park that is just a couple of miles from the hospital. It was the greatest effort for the least return I had ever experienced. I would push and push and barely go anywhere. Not only did I not have the strength or energy, but I also had no idea what I was doing. She kept encouraging me, but at the end of the day, I had gone a little over a mile and she had pushed me half of the way.

"Don't worry, Trish. These things all take time, but you will learn how to do them if you just stick with it. I will help you as much as I can, but you will just have to practice when you get out of the hospital," she said.

I took a deep breath. I was tired of learning and practicing. Starting everything over from scratch was taking a toll on me. I was ready to have something come easily to me. So when Claire suggested swimming, I thought, *That's exactly what I need!*

If there was one thing that my siblings and I shared, it was my mom's command that we all learn to swim. "I never learned how to swim, and I have always regretted it," my mom would say. She loved going to water aerobics and exercising with the ladies at the summer club, but she would never go underwater or step foot in the deep end because she didn't feel she had the skill to keep herself out of trouble. She didn't want that for us, and as each of us got old enough to enter lessons, she had us at the side of the pool, ready to shove us off on the instructor.

I had my first swim lesson when I was four years old and was swimming competitively at the age of seven. I was a pretty hot little swimmer at eight years old, always winning the 25-breaststroke. I continued swimming through summer club and was one of the top freshmen on my high school swim team. I didn't have the motivation or talent to make it on my college team, but I could definitely hold my own in the water, making me very confident when Claire took me downstairs to the therapy pool at Craig. My mom came along to watch. I think she was looking for the same kind of relief I was—and holding on to the hope that I was finally going to find something that allowed me to excel.

Claire helped me transfer onto the lift, which was a chair that would rotate from the deck into the pool and then lower you into the water. The water was much warmer than the competition pool I was used to, but the sensations running through my body were the same. The excitement built in me as Claire helped me slide off the lift and into the water. She held me under my shoulders and had me float on my back for a minute while I got used to being in the water, but I was anxious to show off my swimming prowess (so I thought), so I had her help me turn over so I could swim the length of the pool freestyle. Just as she turned me over and let go, I took one stroke and didn't take one more. I started to sink. Since I was such a competent swimmer before, I had never had this sensation. I started to panic. I was losing my breath and was just praying that Claire would notice my distress and pull me up. It seemed like minutes, but just when I didn't think I could hold my breath a second longer, Claire helped me to the surface. I was in shock and not sure what to think, so I asked her to help me try again. As she turned me over, the same thing happened. My hips flexed, my legs spasmed and the dead weight of my lifeless legs sunk me like there was an anchor tied around my waist. Again I struggled and again Claire pulled me to the surface. It wasn't a fluke. I couldn't swim. "Forget it! Get me out of the pool. I don't want to do this anymore!" I yelled at Claire.

"Trish, you just got in. Give it a chance," she pleaded.

"No. Get me out. I'm not a swimmer anymore. I can't do it and I don't want to do it and I'm never going to bother getting in the water again!" I answered.

She did what I asked while giving my mom a look like *I don't know what else to do...*

I got in my chair and hurriedly pushed back to the elevator and the third floor. I transferred to my bed and put my head in the pillows and cried.

* * *

When I was first injured, my mom and Andy called my friends to tell them about my accident. My mom called Tracey, my college roommate and one of my closest friends. Tracey and I had been friends since freshman year in college and I used to bring her home to Colorado from Vermont, where I went to school my first two years of college. Over spring break, we'd go up to our family cabin and go skiing. Even after I transferred to another school, we remained close and she kept coming to Colorado to ski. We also learned to wind surf and snow board together. She was one of my "active" vacation partners. When my mom got in touch with Tracey and told her that I had been in a bad accident she said, "I don't think you guys are going to be able to go on your ski trips anymore."

When Tracey came to visit for the first time after the accident, I remember being so nervous to see her—wondering what she would think of me. I felt almost embarrassed having her see me sitting in a wheelchair and being a fraction of the independent, self-sufficient person that she knew me to be. I was afraid of having to look up at her and have her looking down on me. But when she came, it wasn't like that at all. She gave me a hug and sat down on the edge of my bed, getting to my level, and asked me how I was doing. We marveled at the fact that we had been through this before with Aldenys. It was odd that two friends on the same dorm floor could end up experiencing the same fate. We talked about how we *were* going to ski together again. It ended up being a good visit, and I was glad to have her there. A spinal cord injury is interesting. It changes a lot of things. It changed a lot of my friendships. Some people turned and ran. Some grew closer. Some didn't know what to make of things, but stood nearby. Tracey was one who never wavered.

Another good friend, Sandy, came to visit shortly after Tracey. She was one of my sorority sisters at the University of Maryland, where I transferred my junior year in college. Before she arrived, I had that same heart-pounding worry that things would be different. Sandy and I also had many active vacations together and I wasn't sure how the visit would go. One day while she was visiting, we were sitting on my bed laughing and gossiping like we often did in our room at the sorority house, when someone knocked on the door. "Come in!" We yelled, giggling because we thought it would probably be the nurse coming in to check on me. But in walked Melanie. The room was silent as she just stood in the corner and looked at me.

Melanie was the friend I was with on the morning of my accident. That weekend, I had gone to Grand Junction with her, her date, Matt and Paul to go to a wine festival. On the way home, we drove in two separate cars. Melanie and her date rode in her car, and Paul, Matt and I in my car. We were going to come back to Denver to go to a bar and watch the football game. On the way home, Melanie called my cell phone and said, "We've decided to skip the game we're just going to go home. I'll talk to you later." That was the last time we talked before the accident that afternoon. After she heard the news, she came one time to visit in the ICU, but stayed a very short time and all but ran out of the room. This was the first time I'd seen her in at least three months. She stood meekly in the corner. I introduced her to Sandy and explained that Sandy was a sorority sister. Melanie was in our same sorority, although she had gone to a different college. I had met her through our local alumna group and we had become fast friends. As she stood in the corner against the wall, she said, "I'm sorry I haven't been to visit you, but it's just so depressing in this place. It's hard to look at you like that and see all the other patients like that too." Sandy and I just gave each other that look like, *Is she really saying this?* We let her go on, and then just like that, she was gone. I had nothing to say. She didn't ask me how I was or how I was dealing with the situation. She didn't walk over and give me a hug or offer a kind word. She basically told me my life was depressing, and that I wasn't much use as a friend anymore and she walked out. I never saw her again.

PART II
ENDURANCE

"Endurance is one of the most difficult disciplines, but it is to the one who endures that the final victory comes."

—Buddha

Chapter 8

Finally in the first week of January, Dr. Lanig came in and told me the news: "You have two weeks left and then you're free. Your discharge date is January 26." The news was good, but overwhelming. I would be going out in the "real world" where I wouldn't have the daily doctor visits to see how I was doing, or the nurses who took care of me and soothed me in times of distress. Instead of being in the majority and having people in wheelchairs all around me like in the hospital, I would be the minority. I was going back to the world of the walking and I wasn't going to be one of them.

My family and I also had to do some quick thinking. Before the accident, I had been living in my dad's house, the house where I spent my teenage years. Andy and I had been sharing the house and taking care of it while my dad had moved to Lamar, Colorado for work. It was a great setup because it was rent-free living in a beautiful house that was a complete comfort for me, having lived there since I was in seventh grade. But the house was all stairs, narrow doorways and otherwise inaccessible in every way. Clearly, I couldn't go home. But I also didn't have any furniture or household accessories of my own since I had lived in a fully furnished home for the past year. I called a high school friend who was a real estate agent and my mom and I hit the road, looking at places.

Since I didn't know what my future with work or income was going to be, we were looking blindly at places, not knowing what price range to stay within or which location would be best. The houses that seemed reasonably priced for me would all require serious retrofitting and wouldn't be practical with a lawn to mow and snow to shovel. We looked at condos and town homes. I needed something that was on the first floor and easy to get around. After two days of going in and out of the car (good practice for my transfers), we found a place, put down a quick offer and within days, I was buying my own condo where I would live alone when I was discharged from the hospital. My mom wasn't sure about sending me home by myself, but at the time of the accident, she and Fred were in the process of moving to the mountains two and a half hours away, Andy was still taking care of my father's house and there weren't any other family members in a position to come and live with me. But I had to have a place and have it immediately, so we made it happen.

It wasn't the same season when I left the hospital as it had been when I went in. Heck, it wasn't even the same year! It was a bittersweet feeling as I left the comfort zone of Craig and went, literally, into the cold world where I had to face the realities of my new life. The beautiful fall days had given way to winter, and white flakes blanketed the grounds of the hospital and swirled in the air as Andy and I hovered against the wind, under the carport of the hospital's exit. I was still far from being an expert at transferring into the car, and Andy could do little to help, but we managed to pile me into the front passenger seat.

Since I didn't yet have possession of the new furniture that I purchased for the condo in a whirlwind shopping spree, I had to spend my first night out of the hospital back in my inaccessible house and inaccessible room. Both terribly difficult reminders of the life I left behind when I rode away from my house on that fateful Sunday afternoon. When Andy and I arrived at the house, we came through the garage, which was the most accessible route despite the two steps we'd have to climb to get into the house. We were both using new skills that we had learned in the hospital about how to get the wheelchair around in situations that were less than ideal. I backed up to the step and Andy leaned me back in a wheelie and pulled me up one step and then the other. At the top of the second step, I wheeled around, and I was at home. Only, it didn't feel like home. It wasn't the same and neither was I. A chill went through my body when I realized that I really couldn't go back and that like it or not, I had a whole new chapter opening in my life.

I felt constrained. There was no place that I could go. The

first-level powder room bathroom was narrow and had a door that
only a standing, walking person and not an overweight one at
that, could get through. There were two flights of stairs up to my
bedroom, as well as two down to the basement TV room. There
was plush, forest green carpet that was like pushing my chair
through mud.

Andy and I turned on the television and sat in the living
room because there was nothing else to do. My life had come to a
standstill, and there wasn't anything compelling me to jumpstart
it at that moment. So, I sat, and thought *This is it. This is where
I am, but I don't know where this leaves me or what I have to look
forward to.*

After hours of feeling like a foreigner in my own house,
Andy and I decided it was time to get me up twenty steps to get
to my bedroom. There was no way he had the strength alone
to pull me up in the chair as we had done from the garage, and
it was just the two of us, so we decided that I would get out of
my chair, sit on the first step and push myself up backward to
the top. Having just come out of the hospital, I didn't have the
strength I needed to do it alone, so Andy would lift my legs as I
did push-ups with my arms to get my butt up one step at a time.
We could only do about two steps in succession before we were
both winded. Long gone were the days when I would fly up ten
steps, swing around the banister and attack the other ten, ending
up in my bedroom in a matter of about ten seconds. This was a
trying exercise for both of us, but in my mind it was more than
just about getting up the steps. It was a foreshadowing of the

struggles I would face from this day forward.

By the time we reached the top step, we were spent. But then, Andy had to find the strength to lift me from the ground back into the chair, which was yet another challenge for our already overworked selves. Lifting with every ounce of strength he had, Andy got me, cockeyed, halfway into my chair, and I was able to shakily lift and right myself the rest of the way. Fortunately, the door to my room was wide enough for me to get through, and I could have one more night in the room I had lived in since seventh grade. I couldn't get into the bathroom, of course, so a shower was out until the next day at the condo, but for once, only needing a catheter and a bottle to pee in was going to work in my favor.

My room was just as I left it—clothes and cycling jerseys strewn about. My bag from the weekend at the wine tasting festival, lay unpacked on the floor. A book lay face down and open on my nightstand, at the same page I left it. A written phone message from Andy was on my desk. I felt like I had gone back in time. Yet everything was different. My life had changed without warning or permission. I was there to spend the night, a visitor in my old world. It no longer belonged to me, or I to it.

* * *

Andy and Greg worked hard to pack up all of my belongings at the house, and brought them to the condo. I had also acquired a room full of stuff from my four months in the hospital. The furniture arrived and was placed in the appropriate places, but the rest of the condo looked like a disaster area. And I was all alone to unpack and set up my new home.

It was so quiet in my house. No more doctors, nurses or friends visiting. No more call button to push when I needed help. I was on my own. No matter how many people would say, "I'm here for you," I knew—this was my battle and my battle alone. Sure, there were people to talk to and support from all angles, but at the end of the day, this was my burden to carry. I'd look in the mirror at my legs that had become atrophied, and they looked out of place. They weren't the cyclist's legs I was used to seeing. I went from being five-foot-ten to four-foot-nothing. I looked up at the shelves at the top of my closet. *Guess I won't be using those.*

Unpacking was the slowest process ever. I would take one or two things out of a box and put them on my lap. Then I'd have to push through the carpet, which felt like molasses, and put the items away. Then back to the box to do it all over again. It took an hour just to empty one box, and I had stacks. Finally, when I couldn't take it anymore, I called the best home organizer I knew, Andy, and asked him for help. I was starting to realize that being in a chair was going to require the use of many new skills for me. Among them, patience, trust and sucking up my pride to ask for help.

My days were a struggle because I didn't know who I was or where I belonged. I wasn't sure who to talk to or what to say.

My family in 1974
Back row: Greg, Andy,
Sam
Front row: Me, Mom
and Dad

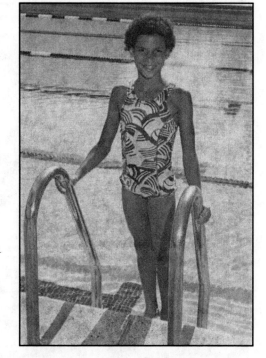

My 8-and-under
swim team picture

Showing off my gymnastics skill, age 10

Me and my brothers
Back row: Andy, Greg, Front row: Sam, James

Racing in a criterium in Denver (I am in the front left corner)

Racing in Wisconsin with Matt, Steve and Paul

My bike after being hit by the car

Me, after being hit by the car

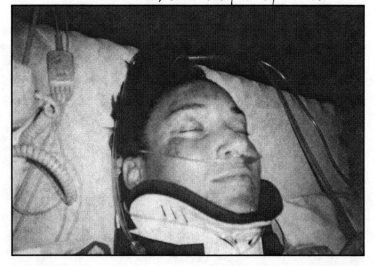

My family came to support me in the Las Vegas Marathon in 2003

Back row: Stepdad Fred, Sam, nephew Jeff, Andy, cousin Tim, Dad
Middle row: Mom, sister-in-law Leigh, niece Katy, Stepmom Susan
Front row: Greg, Me, James

Me in my racing chair

Me in my handcycle

Steve and me

Chapter 9

Friday, March 10, 2001—journal entry

Something that usually starts my day off right and makes me anxious to get out of bed is birds chirping on a blue-sky, sunny day. Today is one of those days, but I'm still feeling the weight of my world. I feel my typical dread of getting out of bed because I know the struggle that lies in front of me...and that's just getting ready for the day.

I can't even begin to think about my day, good or bad, until I'm through with my morning routine. Some days it takes five minutes just to do the transfer out of bed. It's still so hard to believe that I'm me and this is my life. I'm not happy, or even content, and I'm wondering if I ever will be. Will I learn to live like this? Will I ever learn to like, respect and appreciate myself again? These are burning questions in my mind. How can you live without respecting yourself or without being able to be who you are? There is a long road unfolding in front of me and I don't know if I am up for the challenge. My body hurts, my soul is in agony. Yet for now, I will push forward...slowly and miserably, to see if I can see a light at the end of the tunnel. I hope that there I find meaning and reasons that make the struggle seem worthwhile.

Thursday, March 22, 2001

Again I woke up today wondering why I had to have had the accident. This still doesn't feel like my life. I also still feel like I'm floating with no real meaning. I don't have my usual goals or focus and that is very bothersome to me. I don't feel at all like riding a handcycle or pushing a racing chair. Another issue these days is my fatigue. I'm ALWAYS tired. I'm not sure if it's depression or if I'm not sleeping well or what. I hate my physical lack of health. Everything in my body either hurts or doesn't work well or something. I'm not sure how people go on and live like this for years and years. I certainly don't want to be like this forever.

Maybe I should move or change my life. I feel like I need to get out, but then I'm thinking I'd probably be unhappy wherever I went. That is an unpleasant feeling and not really like me. But then, I'm really not me anymore...I'm a new person and it's a person I do not like or respect. That's a hard thing to live with.

Sunday, April 1, 2001

Today is supposed to be a good day. It's usually one of

my favorites. We spring the clock forward so now there's more daylight. More time to ride bikes and enjoy the outdoors. I'm trying hard to see the bright side of the day, but all I feel is alone— another long day with no plans. This is a hard one for me. Hard to keep my mind off of my life, which to me is in its most unhappy moments ever.

Wednesday, April 18, 2001

Ever since our beautiful, sunny Easter day, I've been in the dumps. Usually the sun gives life and energy, but I've had too much life sucked out of me to get it back. All I want to do everyday is get on a bicycle. I want my old life back. It was fine the way it was. I'm not fond of the new life. I'm not sure I have the desire to try and make something of it. It just sucks!

Chapter 10

When I was in the hospital, a friend told me about a charity marathon program where you raise money for the American Diabetes Association while training for a marathon, and then you get to go do the race. It sounded like a fun experience and since my college roommate and good friend Jenn had died from complications of that disease, I thought it would be a perfect goal to shoot for. The only problem was, at that time I was still lying flat from my skin surgery and had yet to sit even one minute in a racing chair. I had no idea how to push a chair or how long a 26.2-mile marathon race would feel using only my arms. But, as with most things, I usually decide what I'm going to do first and figure out the details later. So I signed up. And then I asked as many of my friends as I could to join me on Team Diabetes (Team D). We had to raise $4,500 each, and then we would fly to Hawaii to participate in the Kona Marathon. I did most of my fundraising from my hospital bed, and when I got out in January, I had until June to train and get in shape. I wasn't motivated physically or mentally, so I didn't do much training, but race day was going to come around eventually. My five friends and I met in San Francisco and boarded a flight to Kona and I got my first taste of the hassles of traveling in a wheelchair. I boarded completely dehydrated because I wasn't sure what the protocol would be if I had to go to the bathroom during the flight. When I checked in, I told the gate agent that I would need assistance to my seat. "Well, can you at least walk a few steps?" she said to me in a cranky tone.

"No," I tried to match her bitchiness.

"Well, we'll have to order an aisle chair," she said in an exasperated manner. Not a good way to start your first travel experience in a chair.

Eventually, the attendants came with the aisle chair and I had to transfer into this skinny little chair on wheels that could be maneuvered down the aisle of the plane. They strap you to the chair with three different seatbelts and treat you like you are totally helpless. It was like being on a dolly and I felt like a piece of luggage. Then, they take you to your seat and drop you off. When we got to Kona, same drill. Things didn't get much better because once we got to our hotel, my travel companions wanted to go down to the pool to sit out in the late afternoon sun. As I lay on my lounge chair, I couldn't help but feel jealous as I watched my friends swim and splash in the water. They'd jump in the pool and get out and sun for a bit and then jump back in. I knew that even if I could swim, each one of those very activities would be a major workout in itself. Getting into the water without a lift would mean getting out of my chair to the ground and then scooting into the water. To get out, I had no idea how to lift myself out of the pool and hadn't perfected the transfer from the ground to the chair. My friends tried to take turns staying out of the water to keep me company, but I still had to fight to choke back tears. I was no longer one of them. I didn't know who I was or where I belonged, but it wasn't here.

When race day came, it was a different story. It seemed somehow the playing field had leveled just a bit. I was going to be able to do the same race on the same course as my girlfriends. By this time, I had opted to do the half marathon like a couple of the other girls and the rest did the full marathon. I had a long morning in front of me, but I was there and capable of competing, which I loved. They sent the wheelchair racers off first, and although I got left in the dust by the other wheelers, I felt proud of myself for making it that far.

The 13.1-mile race took me two hours and forty minutes, which is incredibly slow for a wheelchair racer—but I made it. (To give you an idea of times, I now do a full marathon in less than two and a half hours, and the fastest women in the world can do a marathon in under two hours!) As I crossed the finish line, I thought *I can't believe what a fun race that was! Now, this is something I could get excited about!*

That evening, there was a celebratory luau for all the Team

D'ers. There was a program onstage with officials from the ADA telling the crowd how much money we raised as a group and what a successful race it was. After that, they announced to the crowd that I had been the first wheelchair racer to participate on Team D and that I had completed my very first half marathon. The crowd erupted with clapping and whistling and gave me a standing ovation. In that moment, I was able to reflect on what I had been through and how far I had come.

My feeling of exhilaration was short lived. The next day, one of my friends had made reservations for all of us to go on a boat trip. They'd take us out in the ocean and you could dive off the boat and play in the water, and on board there was drinking and hanging out. She had been told over the phone that the boat was accessible, but of course when we got there, it wasn't. After they made a huge deal out of the fact that I was in a wheelchair and there was no way to get me on the boat, two of the workers took me out of my chair and carried me onto the boat, which felt extremely humiliating. When I got on, I realized that there was an upper deck, which I was not going to be able to access, and a bathroom, which was too small to get into. Since it was an all-day cruise with drinking involved, I knew there was no way I could do without a bathroom. I opted to get off the boat. A couple of my friends got off the boat with me, but the rest stayed on to enjoy the cruise. It was yet another reminder of not only what I had lost, but how this was my own weight to bear. As soon as I could, I got on the phone and changed my plane ticket so I could leave Hawaii sooner rather than later. I was done.

* * *

When I got back from Hawaii, I felt like there was hope out in front of me, but it still seemed like it was always just a little bit out of reach. I felt the spark that came with physical exertion and racing, but I still couldn't get out of my funk long enough to really do anything about it. My bike racing friends were off living the life I used to love and it was hard to see them or talk to them about racing. I tried to go watch some races, but every time, my heart felt like it would sink into my shoes. I'd even see random people riding along the bike path and burst into tears while I was driving. I didn't get on my handcycle or racing chair for the rest of that year. I just couldn't. But after watching my friends splashing and playing in the water in Hawaii, I knew there was one thing that I did need to revisit. I called Claire at Craig Hospital and said, "Claire, remember how I told you I was never going to swim again?"

"Yes," she said slowly.

"Well, I guess I was just mad that day. Do you think you could help me try again?"

"Of course I can," she said happily. "Let me know when you can come over and we'll do it."

The next day, I showed up at her office and she walked with me over to the pool. We went through the same steps as the time before: transfer over to the lift and into the pool.

"This time, we're going to take it slow and start from the beginning, okay?"

"Yeah," I said reluctantly.

She put me on my back and held me underneath my shoulders. She pulled me through the pool gently so I could see how my body reacted to the water and change in temperature. We tried different floatation devices and exercises where I would hold onto the side of the pool with one hand and practice stroking with the other. I lowered my expectations and pretended I was swimming for the first time.

"Let's try a few strokes," Claire said. We both decided that I might have a better chance being able to do that staying on my back, so that's what I did. I did a few strokes with her holding on to me, and then she let go and I swam all the way to the other side. The pool was only about twenty feet across, but I figured if I could just master that short distance, I could build on it later. I did a few more laps and then I grabbed on the side of the wall and looked at Claire with the biggest smile I'd had since I left the hospital. "I'm back in business! I did it!"

She just let out a laugh in return. We both knew I just needed to get over that hump and I'd be able to swim as far as I wanted.

* * *

I was beginning to realize that if I wanted to see changes in my life, I was going to have to decide where I wanted to go and what I wanted to do. And then it was up to me to make it happen. One of my cycling teammates, who I didn't know very well before

my accident, ended up being instrumental in my swimming
progression. When I told her about my recent swim lesson and my
desire to get better, she told me of a pool near her that had a lift.
She said she enjoyed swimming in the off-season and offered to
meet me at the pool a couple of times a week to help me practice. I
immediately took her up on the deal, and we met in the evenings.
In the beginning, I could only swim a couple of laps, but each
time we went, I added another lap or two to my workout. I was
beginning to feel comfortable and confident again in the water.

At the same time, my cycling friend, Paul, was providing
the same sort of support to me on my handcycle. I still wasn't very
good at the transfer on and off the bike and was concerned about
going out alone and running into problems, so he rode hours and
miles with me, going at speeds so slow I'm sure he had to work
just to keep his bike upright. But he was patient with me and
never complained about being bored or having to ride slowly.

To learn more about my racer so I could do more road racing
like I did in Hawaii, I decided to attend a wheelchair racing camp
at the University of Illinois that took place in June of 2002. Since
there weren't any local wheelchair racers to learn from, I figured
I could go to camp and get some good pointers about racing in the
chair. And besides that, I loved summer camp when I was a kid,
why not as a 33-year-old?

In 1994, I had gone to graduate school at Eastern Illinois
University and had often made trips to Champaign-Urbana and
the University of Illinois to visit the libraries, which offered many
more volumes of information than the one at EIU, so traveling

back to that campus was not only a nostalgic trip, but one that would also open me up to a whole new world. As I pushed into the dorm and saw all kinds of kids half my age, I wondered, *What am I doing here?* But I knew it was important for me to have at least some instruction on this new machine if I was going to have any kind of racing career. When we met for the first session, I looked around at the six or so kids in my group and realized immediately what an anomaly I was, but also the things I could learn from these young but wise souls. Each one of those kids appeared to have disabilities that they were born with, which means they didn't know the difference between being in a chair and being labeled "disabled." The thing that struck me was that they were no different than any other kid. They were playful and silly with each other, the boys flirted with the girls, and they were there to learn, practice and to race. I envied their seeming security with their bodies and themselves. I wanted to fit in and get on their wavelength. I didn't want them to see me as an adult, as the teacher, and funny enough, they let me in on their teenage games and conversations. In all my insecurity, I was actually able to fit in quite well. Well, at least *I* thought so.

In camp, we learned techniques and did drills. We had practice races and learned how to take care of our bodies, both as athletes and as those with special physical challenges. We did most of our workouts on the track, which were short distance and explosive, sprint-type training. New to the sport and thinking myself more of an endurance athlete, I couldn't keep up with the kids, but I learned enough in those few days that I felt more confident about what was to follow that weekend.

I left Illinois on a Thursday and drove north to Duluth, Minnesota, to visit with my long-time friend, Stacey. Stace had talked me into joining her in a race in the town where she lives. This wasn't just any race, but a full marathon—26.2 miles and I didn't feel ready for a mile of it. I had trained slightly more for this race than the half marathon in Kona, but I still knew I had no business trying to push that far. But it seemed like another good way to advance in my new life and a step closer to getting back to where I was before my accident. So I went.

We woke up to gray skies and chilly, drizzly weather. I had to say goodbye to Stacey in the parking lot because the wheelchairs went in separate busses to the start line than the able-bodied racers. Our start time was a little bit earlier and we started in front of the pack. On the bus, I felt insecure and terrified as I listened to the other athletes rattle off all the races they had done already that season and had planned for the near future. I was clearly outclassed. I sat on the bus and kept to myself. I just listened and tried to learn what I could from the seasoned veterans. Finally, the bus pulled over and we unloaded at a spot just down the road from the start line. We would get in our race chairs, get our gear ready and then push the half-mile or so to the start to get ready for the race. I had to continually remind myself that this was a new sport to me, but I had plenty of racing experience. I knew that once the gun went off and I settled into race mode, I would feel much better. I lined up at the back of the wheelchair field and thought, *Here we go...let's race!*

As it turned out, the field pulled away from me in an instant and I found myself pushing at the very back with only a couple of the straggling racers in sight. There were four female wheelchair racers competing and the first two had totally taken off and were out of my sight. But there was one who I could keep an eye on. I watched her stroke and paid attention to her speed. I used her as my rabbit and worked to catch up with her. I also watched the mile markers as they counted me through the race. One mile down, two miles, three miles. Finally, at about the eight-mile mark, I began to catch my rabbit. *Wow*, I thought. *Maybe I could get third place if I can keep up with this gal.* From then on, we leap-frogged with each other. She'd get back in front of me and then I'd pass her, then be passed. I was surprised that I could keep up and it made the race go quickly. I couldn't believe it when I started getting into the teens, and then I hit the twenty-mile mark. *My arms haven't fallen off yet! I'm hanging in the race!* I felt so proud.

When we got to the end, I started to wear down. The other gal seemed to still be hanging in with me and she looked a lot stronger than I felt. In the last half-mile, I ran out of gas and she pulled ahead to the line to finish just a handful of seconds before me. I didn't mind, though, because not only was I dog-tired, but I had just finished my first marathon, pushing the entire way with my arms! And my time was faster in this race than my time in Kona when I went only half the distance. How could I not be happy with my performance? That night, Stacey had a party at her house and everyone made a toast to my accomplishment. The competition bug had bitten me again and I was ready for more.

When I got home, I started thinking about other races I could do. I thought I would want to race handcycles, but most of the handcycle races in Denver were run in conjunction with the regular able-bodied race events and that would mean going to events where I'd be swamped by people riding bikes, racing the way I used to. The way I still longed to race. I didn't want to put myself into situations that would drag me back down into the hole that I finally felt I was emerging from. I wanted to start in a new direction and do something just a little bit different.

It was then that I remembered the triathlon that Larry and I had done together. Despite being one of the most painful athletic events I had ever entered, it was a lot of fun. I liked the variety of sports involved and the challenge of the event. Besides that, I had been working on my swimming and handcycling up to this point and now with camp behind me, I knew a lot more about how to push a wheelchair. And with that, the idea to do a triathlon was born.

Who else could I call, but Larry, my triathlon buddy? I knew he would support me in this effort and by that time, he had competed in an Ironman, which is really the pinnacle event of the sport. An Ironman is a 2.4-mile swim, followed by a 112-mile bike and a 26.2-mile run. I figured if he could do that, he wouldn't mind joining me for a short sprint race, and plus, he could give me some good tips and pointers.

My next challenge was to find a race to do. Since Colorado is full of races, it wasn't hard to find a sprint triathlon. There was one in Fort Collins, Colorado, which is just about an hour north of Denver. The distances were a 450-yard swim, 12-mile bike and a 3-mile run. It sounded doable to me. Afterall, I had just completed a marathon and I was sort of feeling like a big stud. I got on the phone and called the race director to ask him if he would allow me to participate in his race. When he answered, I said, "Hi, my name is Trish Downing and I'd like to do your triathlon. First, though, the reason I'm calling is that I am in a wheelchair and I didn't want to catch you off-guard when I showed up."

The other end of the line was silent.

I kept talking, "You see, I have learned how to swim and I ride a three-wheeled bike called a handcycle. For the run, I will use my racing chair, which looks just like the ones that racers use in the Boston Marathon. I can do all the sports required: I just do them a little differently. I'd like to try them in my first triathlon."

"Uh...okay. But I don't know anything about this. Can you bring your own support crew to help you with the race?" he asked.

"Sure. No problem. I'll see you next weekend."

Larry and I headed up to Fort Collins the day before the race. We went to the race site and checked out the transition area. "Transition" as it's called, is the place where you change between sports. After the swim, you go into transition to put on your bike shoes and helmet and grab your bike to begin the second leg of the race. When you are done with the bike, you go back into transition, ditch your bike, shoes and helmet put on your running shoes and head out on the last leg of the race. It's important to know the transition area, where the entrances and exits are (they are usually different for the bike and the run) as well as the course. Larry and I drove the course and checked out the footpath where the run would be. We figured out a race strategy so that my handlers (the people who help you in a race) would know what to do and how to help me.

The next day, I had the undivided assistance of Larry and four other friends who had come to help me with my race. I was so nervous because I didn't know what to expect from my first triathlon in a wheelchair, and also, I didn't want to make a fool of myself in front of 350 able-bodied athletes.

The swim was in an indoor pool, and as I was rolling around the deck and looking at all the tanned and fit bodies, I started to get self-conscious. My own insecurity translated every glance into a piercing stare that said, *You don't belong here.* I was sure they were wondering what a woman in a wheelchair was doing in a swimming suit and at a triathlon. I longed for my former body, that of a cyclist, but I knew that wasn't to be. Like it or not, this was the new me and I had a race to do.

The race started with a 450-yard swim in a time trial format. That meant that all the racers lined the perimeter of the pool and would start the swim one at a time. We went off in five-second intervals and swam in a snake swim. Each person would go up one lane and down the next, then up the next and down the next, until they worked their way across the whole pool and exited out at the opposite corner. When the competitor got to the far side of the pool, they would get out, run outside into transition, hop on the bike and be off. I was the last athlete in line because we were seeded by speed and of course, I was the slowest. I was the tail of the snake. But as I looked up in the bleachers at all the spectators, I felt more like the butt of a joke. *Do I really belong at this race?* When it was my turn, one of my support crew friends gave me a little push to help me off the wall and into the water. I turned over on my back and started stroking. My friends split up so they were on both sides of the pool and every time I got to the wall, I could look up at them jumping up and down and cheering for me. It got me thinking of a time in high school when I had sprained my ankle just a day before a big swim meet. I had no choice but to race because we needed all the points we could get. I had to dive off the blocks and push off the walls with just one foot. The other one was in excruciating pain. My teammates knew I had to dig deep to be able to race that day, so they crowded the ends of the lanes and every time I got to the wall, they had a chant for me, "Trish, Trish the crippled fish!" It was so funny to us at the time and in this first wheelchair triathlon, I had to chuckle at the irony. I sang the cheer to myself during the swim and couldn't help but give myself a little laugh inside.

The swim took me three times longer than any of the other racers and when I finished, I looked up at the bleachers. Empty. I scanned the pool deck. Empty, except for the five friends I brought to help me with the race. They helped me out of the water and pushed me in my chair outside to the transition area. All of the bikes were gone. Every one of the other racers was out on the course. I was the last person to go.

The bike course was three laps of four miles each. Twelve

miles total. My first lap was great. Although my arms felt totally spent from the swim, the other racers were starting to warm up to me. Almost everyone gave me a cheer as they rode past. "Go wheels!" "You can do it!" "It's so great you're out here racing!" It filled me up with excitement to have so many people cheering for me. But when I got to the second lap, there were fewer people out there, and I was getting passed by rookies with flat pedals and their helmets on backwards. By the third lap, I was out there all alone. As I rode along, I began to feel disheartened. Racing was fun...when there were other people around. But out there by myself, I felt left out. Lonely. Another reminder that things just weren't quite the same in my life. I started feeling sorry for myself and thinking, *I'm not an athlete anymore...I don't belong out here.* Then I remembered a bike race that I did one time when I had not eaten well before the race and I bonked in the middle and, like they say in cycling, I got "dropped like a bad habit" from the pack. I was riding alone and this racer from one of the other categories rode up next to me and she asked me, "How's your race going? How are you doing today?"

I told her, "I suck! I'm just having the worst day." And she said, "You know, you can't let just one race define who you are as an athlete. You can only do what your body can do on a given day." She told me to "ride my own race."

That thought came rushing back to me as I rode alone in the triathlon and I thought to myself, *Ride your own race. You're doing this with your arms and everyone else is doing it with their legs.* That got me through the bike ride, but when I got back into transition, there were still no bikes. I immediately realized what that meant. Everyone else had not only finished the race, but had vacated the premises. They were probably all at home with their feet up, drinking a beer, and I was still in the middle of the race! My friends were there for me again and helped me out of the handcycle, into my everyday chair and then over into the racing chair. My body was spent and I was feeling sorry for myself. As I pushed off, I reminded myself to *ride my own race*. As I was pushing my chair, looking down at the cracks in the sidewalk and just trying to get through the race, I looked up and in front of me I saw a healthy, albeit tired, able-bodied straggling runner and I thought *Dude, you're doing down!* I started pushing with every bit of reserve strength and energy. I caught and passed him, and when I did, I realized a very important fact. I was no longer in last place! I got a renewed sense of purpose and dug even deeper. By the time I reached the finish line, I had passed seven able-bodied racers in total. I raised my arms in victory as I looked into the eyes of my friends and helpers. I had done it! Not only did I finish and I wasn't last, but I proved to myself that I was an athlete again. And I *could* do the things I did before my accident. Just in different ways. The experience opened my eyes and I started to see more possibilities lying in front of me.

Chapter 11

My racing started to take off locally. I entered all the races
I could: 5Ks, 10Ks, sprint triathlons. At one point, someone from
a TV news station got wind of what I was doing and asked for an
interview. I was fine with that, so they shot a story of me at Wash
Park training in my racing chair. It aired on the local nightly
news for all to see. Even Judy, the woman who had hit me with
her car, saw the broadcast.

I wouldn't have known that she watched it, except that
my attorney called me shortly after and told me that he had
something for me. I dropped by his office one day and there he
handed me an envelope. It was from her. Inside was a card. I
opened it slowly, gingerly, not sure what was going to be inside.

Many months before the letter, and almost one year post-
accident, I found myself in a courtroom with the woman who

hit me. I hadn't had any contact with her prior to that meeting, which wasn't actually a *meeting*. We didn't shake hands and say "hi" or anything. It was more of a "viewing" sitting across a courtroom from each other. It was the first time I even got a chance to know what she looked like. At the site of the accident, Matt, in a state of shock, was the one who had contact with her. He had gotten up in her face and yelled at her while I lie on the ground fighting to breathe. A couple of days after the accident, she called the hospital to talk to my mom, but my mom didn't talk to her. She couldn't. What was she going to say to the woman who had quite possibly ruined her daughter's life? Instead, my brother Sam took the call. He is cool-headed and calm and was in a better state to speak to her. He gave her an update on my condition and little else. She called once or twice after that, but the calls quickly dropped off.

When I tell people about the accident and the fact that I was not at fault, so often I hear, "*Well!* I would have *sued!*" It's actually not quite that simple and straightforward. I had an attorney help me with the process of filing a civil suit, but in the end, it was found that Judy, the driver, didn't have any asssets to make a lawsuit worthwhile. In his rudimentary explanation, "You can't get blood from a turnip." This was difficult for me to hear because I had no idea how I was going to pay for my new and much more expensive state of being. But I did have one additional opportunity to hold her responsible for restitution: a criminal trial through the city of Golden. I was asked to come in to give one short testimony, which amounted to about thirty words. My

friend, Liz, accompanied me for support. Prior to the hearing, I
spoke with the state trooper who had been at the accident scene.
He told me he was sure I would win the judgment, as Judy's
defense for hitting me was that the "sun was in her eyes" and "she
didn't see us."

"Technically, if the sun is in your eyes," he said, "you
shouldn't have your foot on the accelerator making forward
movement until you are sure you can see what is in front of you."
He was also going to give that information to the judge, testifying
on my behalf. As we sat in court, Judy's attorney was arguing
that I should have been riding on a bike path rather than the
street and basically insinuating that I caused my own fate. All I
got to do was give a short description of the accident and say that
I had been paralyzed from the chest down. It was over in less
than three minutes. The next day, my attorney called me and told
me I had lost. Judy would receive no more than a traffic citation
for careless driving.

So, the fact that I now had a mortgage payment that
stretched my teacher's salary to the limit, health insurance that
didn't cover the cost of catheters—it was about a dollar and
twenty five cents every time I had to go pee—and nearly weekly
visits to the doctor's office, meant that I was in a difficult spot.

When I got the envelope from Judy via my attorney, my
first thought was that she wanted to help me in some way. I
opened the card and read, "Dear Tricia: I am very sorry for
causing your paralysis..." She went on to tell me that she had
seen me on the news and how good I looked. She praised me for

being an "overcomer."

As I read the letter, I could feel myself getting dizzy with a rush of emotion. I thought, *How dare you?* It felt like after seeing me in a minute and a half story on the TV news, she could disregard every piece of hell I had been through and decide on her own that I was fine. Yes, I was healing and yes, I was forming a new life. But it was still a process and a conscious decision that I had to make every day. At that point, it was still work to wake up every morning with a smile on my face and the desire to get through another day. She told me about her own healing and how God would get her through.

I had no doubt that her situation was difficult. I have often put myself into her shoes and wondered if I would want to face another day, having done what she did. Unfortunately, I think we were both in tough situations. But it didn't make me want to be her friend. It didn't make me more sympathetic or make it easier to forgive. I just wanted to forget and move on with my life.

I actually called Matt that night. We had only talked a handful of times since he left St. Anthony. Our relationship just wasn't strong enough to survive. Everything about our relationship, from day one, was intense, explosive, and powerful. But somewhere in there, we lacked a foundation. Lacked history.

It was good to talk to him, though. Only he could understand the emotions that surrounded the accident itself, the loss and the terror of a beautiful day turned tragic.

"The only way to get her out of your life and your mind is to say how you feel, Trish." You need to get it all out and so do I.

She changed our lives forever and unless we tell her, really let her know, we won't be able to put this behind us."

We decided the best course of action was to write our own letters. And send them to her. So that's what we did.

Dear Judy:

I'm sure this isn't a letter that you want to read. Chances are you want to put this incident out of your mind and forget that it ever happened. Fortunately, you can...if you decide. But for me, every morning I wake up, it's the first thing that comes to my mind. I don't have a choice...it lives with me, every hour of every day. I can't even sit up in bed without thinking about my injuries. Why? I don't have the stomach muscles to just "sit up." I have to roll my body over, one part at a time—legs, hips, upper body—and prop myself up on my elbow, if I have the strength, or tug on the sheets to pull myself up to a sitting position. Yes, all that just to sit up...and that's just the beginning of my day.

I'm sure that for you, September 26, 2001, was a victorious day. "Not guilty." For me, it meant that I alone have to pay for someone else's lack of attention. I pay financially, physically, mentally and emotionally. For a moment, I believed that if a jury could find you "not guilty," maybe they could find me "not paralyzed." No, all I had to do was wake up on a new morning and I would learn that wasn't at all the situation.

I wonder how I will live knowing that in one moment my dream, my body and my life were shattered. How could I—having been following all of the rules of the road, minding my own business, sharing with an out-of-state friend one of my favorite training rides—end up having to pay so dearly for something that wasn't my fault?

I know and understand that this was not a vicious, purposeful attack. But a momentary lack of attention and carelessness has forever changed my life. Can I put this to rest and move on with my life? No, not until I know that YOU know how this has shattered my sense of self—how the person I used to be was destroyed in an instant.

For my whole life, I have wanted nothing more than to be an elite athlete. And five years ago, I finally found my passion... the sport that I would stop at nothing, in which to succeed. I was willing to give it my all...create my whole life around it just for the feeling of satisfaction that I had racing against the top women in the country. Yes, I "put all my eggs in the cycling basket" as they say, and was determined and motivated to give it my very best.

I purposefully found a job that would allow me to have the summer off to race. I auditioned for and received a contract with a local modeling agency to make extra money while I wasn't working my full-time job or racing. Since I am not married and live on my income only, my family supported me in my move back home so that I could live rent-free and afford to race and train as much as I could physically stand. I spent my free time on my bike. I limited my circle of friends to those who understood and shared my passion. With the help of my dad, I purchased what was my idea of the perfect car...four-wheel drive, stick shift, bike racks on top and roomy enough for one friend and a summer's worth of racing gear. In the summer of 2000, I packed it all up and drove across the country for what amounted to eighteen races in 23 days. It was the summer of my life and from the moment I returned home, I began to develop a strategy to improve my training and making plans for the summer of 2001 when I would go back to those races and instead of just participating, I would "make my mark."

I never even considered that one day in between the most notable summer of my life and the year I planned to achieve great things in my favorite sport, I would end up spending four months in the hospital and never walk again. It's a tough thing to take, and ironic that the prized possession of my body, my cyclist's legs, would be rendered helpless. What I worked hours to build—the strength, muscle memory, endurance—no more and never again. That doesn't even include the variety of other problems that come with a spinal cord injury...three-quarters of my body shut down or mildly functioning.

I've paid and will continue to pay dearly for this accident. I couldn't go back home; there were too many stairs, so I had to purchase a new home in which I could make the appropriate modifications. I could no longer drive my brand new car...it couldn't be modified. My dreams and goals a distant memory. Everything that I loved about myself—my spontaneous nature, my independence, athleticism, health, all gone. Who am I now? A fraction of what I was and locked into a person I have no interest in being. The things that made my life worthwhile to me are now only visions in my daydreams. Gone is the day I will walk down the aisle in a long, flowing, white gown. Gone are the days when I'd drop by a friend's house and run up the stairs to give a surprise knock on the door. Gone are the days when I jump in my car and take off on a road trip. Gone are the sunny days I spent riding through town with my friends. Gone are my hopes of playing with my children, doing gymnastics with them in the front yard of my house. Gone are my spirit and my hopes for the future.

I have spent the last year and a half trying to recover what is left of my life. I have had to heal my body, mind and heart in order to get back to work and pay the bills. Each day, I deal with severe back pain and body aches as I sit for eight-to-ten hours at work. I have to smile when all I want to do is cry. I go on because I'm still on this Earth. I go on because I don't have a choice. I don't have someone to take care of me. I don't have someone to pay the bills when I am too tired and sore to work. I go on out of habit and necessity, not desire.

Now is the time for the cycling season. Every cyclist I see reminds me of my disability. Every friend I talk to who tries to keep me informed of the cycling world breaks my heart. My eyes fill with tears on a sunny day. I feel like I'm in a prison, and for something I didn't do.

Sure, a person picks her own attitude. I have done the best I know how. But I've heard it said that "when you give up your dream, you die." What happens if one day you were just robbed of it? In that case, it also breaks your heart. I guess that sums up the life I am left to lead—directionless, broken hearted, and empty. Hardly what you dream about as a kid. Wasted potential. The feeling that I could do ANYTHING I set my mind to is a distant memory.

Maybe someday I will heal...in spirit, that is. My injuries are permanent. Maybe someday it'll be okay not to walk or ride a bike. Maybe someday my life will feel whole again. Maybe...

Tricia Downing

Matt and I were both hurt in the accident. It was, of course, a different experience for the two of us, but the impact was great.

TO: Judy

Since we were never formally introduced, I would like to take this time to introduce myself to you. My name is Matt. I am thirty-three-years old and an electrical engineer. I wanted you to know this because now you have a name and realize I also exist. I was the other cyclist on September 17, 2000 at approximately 6:00 p.m.

Now that you know who I am, I wanted to give you a little background on how that weekend happened. Trish Downing and I met in July at a cycling race in Milwaukee, Wisconsin, and became very close. In fact, fell in love. Now, things were a bit complicated because I was living in Pennsylvania and she lives in Colorado. Trish and I were figuring things out and how to handle this long distance relationship. She decided that being friends was the best option for us. Trish invited me to a wine tasting festival and bike ride in Colorado. This was a weekend event. I decided that this

*would be my final opportunity to see if Trish and I would ever
be involved in a romantic nature. So I flew to Colorado, where
Trish, myself and a few friends went away for the weekend. At
the end of this weekend, I was still undecided on how things were
going to progress. I decided that on the long drive home, I would
not say a word and see how things went. Well, Trish, being Trish,
cannot be quiet for a long time and we started talking. We decided
that during my final afternoon we would go for a nice two- or
three-hour bike ride around one of her favorite routes and her
favorite climb, Lookout Mountain. Well, cycling is how we met
and what we did best together. On this ride, we rode along talking
like we had known each other for thirty years. We laughed and
joked until the climb. Then we began to climb Lookout. It was a
beautiful Sunday afternoon and the weather was perfect for a bike
ride. Instead of climbing as hard as we could, which is what most
cyclists would do, we just peddled, enjoyed the view and talked
until we reached the top. At the top, we stopped to fill our water
bottles and snacked for a second. I'll never forget that moment
for two reasons: First, what attracted me to Trish the first time I
ever saw her was her long perfect athletic legs and great butt. I
vividly remember and will never forget the moment she walked
into this restaurant at the top of the mountain. She had a pair
of cycling shorts on that only we could giggle about, and as she
walked away, I just couldn't keep my eyes off her. When she came
out, she was laughing about something, I can't remember what,
but it doesn't matter because what I witnessed was the last time
she would walk. Second, at the moment she disappeared into the*

restaurant, I decided I was totally and completely in love with her. I planned on telling her exactly how I felt when we got back to her house. I remember the ride down the mountain. She was so excited because she loved to corner around the tight bends. I remember riding past the Coors Brewery and heading down that fateful road. The exact thought that was going through my mind was, "I can't believe I finally found a girl who I get along with so well and who loves to do the same sport I do and has the same passion for it. I can't believe we have so much fun together and I totally love this girl. What a perfect day—this is what being happy is."

The next thing I remember was riding down the street and noticing a white car waiting to turn into a development. I knew we were okay, because the car was not ready to turn yet because it wasn't in the right spot to do it. So we continued on…but the next thing I know, that white car is about to run me over. Out of nowhere, this white car cut across the lane and was accelerating right at us. By the grace of God, I was able to move just a few millimeters enough to get clear. Then, I heard the worst noise I have ever heard. I ended up in the grass and sidewalk, only to turn around to see the girl I was completely head over heals in love with lying on the ground. Her bike was mangled and she wasn't moving. In those next three seconds, I couldn't feel myself move— but the next thing I knew, I was standing in front of a perfectly normal woman, who was standing there next to her white car doing absolutely nothing. NOTHING! I had to scream in her face to call an ambulance. This woman immediately said, "I'm sorry,

I didn't see her, I WAS LOST." But we will get back to that too.
That woman was you.

I stooped over Trish to see if she was alive and the first thing
she said to me was, "Matt, I can't move my legs." Other then her
being dead, she couldn't have said anything worse to me, because
I knew how much she loved to use her legs for all sorts of sports.
For example: Trish was a gymnast. The day before the accident,
she showed me how she could do a running back handspring...
twice. Trish was also an avid swimmer. She worked at the
Olympic Training Center for swimming. Trish was a die-hard
cyclist, but you know that. When she said those words to me, I lost
all the blood in my head. I thought I was going to puke and pass
out, but somehow I just talked to her and tried to help while the
help was on the way.

The next two weeks were a blur. But since you weren't
there, let me fill you in on how it went. We made it to the hospital
and the doctors took over. Now, when you're in this situation,
you always just figure it is bad, but nothing serious. We'll be out
riding in a couple of weeks. One doctor explained to me what
the procedure was and what happens sometimes in these cases—
there was a chance she was just swollen. The next thing I had to
do was inform her family. I wanted to thank you personally for
that. That was an awful thing to have to do. Then I had to sit
in the waiting room while doctors probed and tried to evaluate
Trish. On top of that they tried, UNSUCCESSFULLY, to help
her with the incredible pain she was in. One by one, her family
came in. I didn't have the first clue what to do or say. In fact, I

*thought it was my fault. I still to this day am thankful I wasn't
hit, but I feel guilty that I wasn't hit and Trish was. Why didn't I
stop instead of swerve? Maybe she would have fallen but not been
run over by the white car. Maybe I should have gone slower the
previous few miles...all these things I think about today. As the
hours passed and the doctors came in, we all waited and waited
to hear the news. Finally, the doctor came in and told us the bad
news. She had a severely broken back and neck, broken ribs and
shoulder. But he was very concerned about internal injuries and
her heart. He was very concerned she wouldn't make it through
the night. For the next two days, we waited in the hospital for
signs of improvement. Trish could talk, but wasn't very coherent.
The day came when she needed to go into surgery. Seven or eight
hours later at 2:00 a.m., the doctor came out and delivered the
news. The surgery went well, she would live. But she would not
walk again.*

*Over the next two weeks, I rarely slept or ate. All I wanted
and needed to do was be there for any little thing Trish or her
family needed. It was amazing to see how many friends she had.
They all came to the hospital or wrote letters and emails.*

*Thing is, with a person who goes through what YOU put
Trish through, there are many stages of mental states. None of
which I can possibly understand. One of those stages split Trish
and me and we did not see or talk to each other for over a year.
That is right, a year. Now I am writing this from my perspective,
and will tend to be selfish towards my feelings. I went from
having the happiest day of my life, to complete hell, to two weeks*

of no sleep taking care of Trish, to absolutely no contact. In one split decision by you, you put a girl in a wheelchair for life and took the girl I was in love with away from me. I don't know if we would have ever made it in a relationship, but you never gave us the chance. We talk occasionally now, but it is not and never will be the same.

There are many stories of things that happened in the hospital—the multiple surgeries and pain, and the struggle her family had seeing their daughter/sister in this state of pain and outcome. There are many stories I don't know about the things Trish went through. There are more stories of what I deal with and dealt with over that first year. But you moved on. Well, I think you need to understand a few things first.

First—No one thinks you hit Trish on purpose, but it WAS your fault.

Second—You were on your way to a Bible Study class, according to the trooper who talked to you. You are supposed to be a "good person." But here are the FACTS. 1. You made a turn across traffic, well ahead of where you should have turned. 2. You told both the trooper and me that you were lost and looking for a street. 3. Never once did you tell anyone the sun was in your eyes. 4. You hit an innocent cyclist. 5. Initially, you wanted to help.

Third—Sometime after that, you must have talked to someone who, rightfully, tried to console you. You have apparently convinced yourself you were not responsible for this terrible accident. You have apparently listened to a lawyer who told you not to do or say anything. A jury, not being there at the time, had to let you off because you had a good lawyer, not because you were innocent.

There are only three people who know what and how you did it, Trish, you and I. There was one other person who sees this type of thing all the time, the Trooper. The Trooper told both Trish and I, that you were 100% responsible for the accident. You made the turn not completely knowing what was coming at you. Either you were looking at the sign (we know that to be the truth, don't we? It is what you immediately offered), or the weak story someone planted in your head (and you lied about in court) about the sun being in your eyes. In either case, you made a bad decision to turn across traffic. Only you made that decision. Therefore, only you could be responsible. If you were looking at the road, you would have seen us right in front of you and waited. If the sun was in your eyes, you should have blocked it first. You did neither and you made the turn. End result: you made a bad decision, paralyzed a wonderfully athletic girl and took away any chance we had to have a romantic relationship. By the way, we were riding completely according to the law.

Now, you have run and hidden behind a lawyer. You have hidden so you can move on with your life. You have hidden and lied to prevent you from having to lose any money. By God's will, you are supposed to help when needed; you are not supposed to choose money over the "right thing to do." You are supposed to take responsibility for your actions, whether they were on purpose or not. In your head you have to know you did the wrong thing. In your head, you have to know it is decisions like this that define you as a human being. You have failed.

You need to understand the costs Trish has accumulated and will have to take care of the rest of her life. Her insurance will not cover all that is needed. She pays over $300 a month on top of what her insurance pays for her medicine and incidentals that a person in a chair must deal with every day. That is in today's money. What happens next year or five years from now? I actually have no concept of what she has to do on a daily basis to survive. Mentally, physically and financially, every day is an absolute challenge.

Now, Trish is an incredibly strong person both mentally and physically. She has friends many people only wish they had. But when you ran and hid and the court decided "no fault" by you, it made her feel like she didn't matter. Someone just ran her over and according to YOU, who did it, and the court, it didn't matter—in fact, you and your lawyer tried to make it sound like SHE did something wrong. Neither Trish nor I can forgive you for not taking responsibility for your BAD DECISION. IT WAS 100% YOUR FAULT!!!!

In that instant that I met you face to face, my first thought was to knock you out. For some reason, I did not do it. I knew you didn't do it on purpose. You looked like a good person. I was wrong. Some day you will wake up and realize what you did. You took something away from two innocent people that can never be replaced. And you couldn't even take responsibility. Not only disappointing, but pathetic. I'd also like to add in any and every curse word applicable to you in big bold capital letters. You figure out what they are.

Matt

Chapter 12

The healing process following my accident was a roller coaster of emotion. I had ups, downs, twists and turns. One day would be fine and hopeful. The next day, I'd want to jump off a cliff. I had to get over the resentment and bitterness I felt toward the driver, and writing my "venting" letter went a long way to saying what needed to be said. The rest was just going to take time and patience. It's difficult knowing that even if you do everything right, someone else could come along and screw it all up. Even to this day, it could eat me up if I let it, but I don't. I won't.

Part of my healing process was regaining my independence, and since I am a fairly stubborn and private person, I made that transition quickly. My friends and family were always there when I needed them, but I tried my hardest to need them as little as possible. It also helped to go back to work. As difficult as it was for me physically, I trudged through. It was like climbing a hill in a race. Slow and steady, one little step after another.

Finding another relationship weighed heavy on my mind and in my priorities, but some things you just can't rush. Derrick disappeared from my life shortly after I got out of the hospital, and would reemerge here and there for four years afterwards, but it got tiring dealing with the ebb and flow of his presence.

I often felt like my life had hit a wall, and all the while, I had to sit by and watch my friends' lives as they flowered. Marriages, children, new jobs—it seemed like everyone was moving forward as I treaded water and held on for dear life. I wanted to be happy for them, but I really just felt sorry for myself. The one thing I knew that could save me and did ultimately save me was my passion for sports and competition. I could be having the worst week, but on the weekend when I got to the start line, none of the other stuff mattered. I had a job to do and it was something that I knew and loved. I may not have the race of a lifetime, I might have tough moments in a race, but when I was out there, I was where I wanted to be. Racing is funny; it can break you down and make you crazy. You can fly off the handle and curse like a sailor. Some races are good and some are bad. But over the course of time, it's true that "that which does not kill you makes you stronger." I guess it's really just a microcosm of life.

Sometime in the summer of 2003, I learned about the World Triathlon Championships and its division for physically

challenged athletes. In order to qualify for the race, you had
to complete an Olympic distance race in less than four hours.
When I found out qualifying for this race was open to all athletes
and that the 2003 race was in New Zealand, I immediately
wanted in. I had never done an Olympic distance race, which is a
1.5-kilometer swim, 40-kilometer bike and 10-kilometer run. That
was a little more than twice the distance of the sprint races I had
been doing, but I had enough racing under my belt that I wanted
to give it a try. At the time, I had hired a new triathlon coach
and I was telling her about my goal. We discussed everything
I had done in wheelchair racing up to that time and she was
totally on board with my idea. But when we got to the part about
swimming, she stopped. Since my injury, I had only been able to
swim backstroke. It was the only stroke where I had control of
my body and any sort of speed, which at the time was not much.
When I rolled over on my stomach to swim freestyle, my hips
would close up into a pike position, my legs would spasm all over,
my butt would rise and my head would sink. There was no way
I could stay in a straight streamline position and swim the front
crawl. I never thought it was a problem to settle on doing the
backstroke, and it had worked fine in the pool. This coach stopped
me in mid-sentence as I told her about my swimming and she
said, "There's no way you can do an Olympic distance triathlon
if you're swimming backstroke. All the races that distance and
longer are in open water. You'll never be able to see where you
are going or stay on course."

Her words felt like a sock to the stomach and I was out of

breath with nothing to say. But as I left, I thought, *I'll show her! I don't know how, but I'll figure it out.*

That night, I called my friend and former cycling coach, Kathy, who was also a swimmer and coached triathletes. I told her what the coach had said to me earlier that day and I said, "Isn't there a way I could still swim in the open water even though I only know backstroke?"

After bantering ideas around for several minutes, we realized the answer was as simple as revisiting our past experiences. During the summer of 1998 when I was racing the tandem, Randy and I qualified to race in the World Cycling Championships for the disabled. Kathy was one of the team coaches. That was how we originally met, and how she came to be my personal cycling coach.

"Trish, this isn't much different from when you were a tandem pilot. You were the eyes for someone who couldn't see. Now, you're swimming backstroke and you can't see where you're going. What if another person could be the eyes for you?"

"You mean like having someone swim next to me and point me in the right direction?"

"Yeah. What do you think?"

"Let's try it!"

Kathy and I met at the reservoir and went for a swim. I did my usual backstroke and she swam next to me, yelling directions or pointing which way I needed to go. It worked.

Now all I had to do was find an Olympic distance race to go to before the qualifying deadline. I picked the Chicago Triathlon and Kathy and I headed east to try out our new system.

The Chicago Triathlon is the world's largest triathlon. With over 6,000 entrants, it is quite a production. I had contacted the race director ahead of time because I wasn't sure if there were any other physically challenged athletes that would be doing the race. Since there were so many swimmers, we went off in waves of about 100-150 athletes, with a few minutes between each wave. Kathy and I enlisted the help of some volunteers to lift me out of my chair and literally drop me down into the lake. Then, Kathy had to jump in right after me because without the use of my legs, I couldn't tread water like the rest of the swimmers. Having only done a handful of triathlons and this being such a big race, I was a little out of my element. Kathy suggested that we start at the back of the pack to keep from being run over by the other swimmers. A triathlon start can be pretty intimidating with arms and legs flying everywhere. It isn't uncommon to get kicked or punched or have your goggles knocked off, but we decided that along with providing directional assistance, Kathy would also protect me from the masses since I couldn't kick back to defend myself. More than once, Kathy had to fend off aggressive swimmers and got many dirty looks. Swimming on your back also causes a lot of other problems in addition to not being able to see where you are going. When the water is wavy and rough, it's not an exaggeration to say you can easily ingest the equivalent of a glass or two of water. Every so often during the swim, I had to sit up because I would be choking on the water I drank or I'd need to catch my breath. And the worse my swim, the harder it is for my guide. Kathy kept up with me perfectly, but it was hard for us not to want to wring each other's necks every once in a while. It got heated in the water because of the race pressure and the fact that a wrong move could put one or the other of us in danger. But eventually we made it to the swim finish, and a group of volunteers swept in and got me out of the water. They lifted me into my chair and Kathy helped me get to transition, which was the equivalent of about a block away. She helped me into my handcycle and sent me off on my way. The good thing about this course was that there were so many cyclists and so many waves that I was never on the course alone. I had hundreds of people blowing by me on bikes, but they all yelled and cheered for me as they passed. The thing about being the only wheelchair racer among a group of able-bodied athletes is that everyone notices you. Sometimes, the other racers are inspired, sometimes I know they are feeling sorry for me, but whatever their take on the situation, I'm like the underdog and they want to make sure I know they're with me, if only in spirit, as they cruise by me like I'm standing still.

It took me two and a half hours to finish the bike, so when I got back to transition, Kathy and I both knew I didn't have a second to spare. We did the usual: out of the handcycle to the everyday chair, and then into the racing chair and I was off.

The run was on a wide bike path, but there were still a lot of runners out there. The problem with the racing chair is that it doesn't steer like a bike. You have some small movements you can make with the steering mechanism, or you can bunny hop it around to change direction, but it's not good for playing "dodge the runners." That, coupled with the fact that my skills still needed a little extra work, made for a slightly tenuous run. Plus, I was so exhausted. Back in my cycling days, my favorite races were an hour or less in length, so for me a four-hour race seemed like an eternity. I pushed my heart out in that race, just praying that I could make it across the finish line in less than four hours. When I got to the finish line, I gave one final push, sat up and looked for Kathy, who was keeping tabs on my official time. As soon as I saw her, I gave her that look like, *Well? Did I make it?* She looked at her watch and up at me and I saw a smile creep across her face. "Three hours and fifty-six minutes! You made it by four minutes!" In that moment, my whole body relaxed and I wilted into my chair like a dead flower.

"I'm exhausted!" I said.

"Yeah, but you're going to New Zealand!" Kathy exclaimed.

"You mean *we*. *We* are going to New Zealand, " I said.

"Yeah."

We smiled and high-fived!

* * *

Traveling to New Zealand turned out to be an adventure. Or better put, a misadventure. It seemed like there was a roadblock in every direction we turned. Kathy and I both started from Denver, but we were on separate flights to Los Angeles. I got lucky on my flight and was upgraded to first-class; therefore,

I got to drink free wine the whole way. It seemed like a good idea until we landed and I realized that I was a little bit tipsy. Add to that the fact that my flight was late arriving, and I was, of course the last person off the flight because I had to use the aisle chair. My connection was tight and I had to hustle. Kathy met me at my gate and we blew through the concourse to our next flight. She put her hand on the back of my chair and pushed, carrying the bags and running all at the same time. Out of breath, we made it to our gate just in time. Our first flight took us to Auckland and then we were to jump a small plane to Queenstown. As our airplane landed, the view took my breath away. It was the most gorgeous place I had ever seen. We looked at each other with wide eyes like, *Oh my gosh, we have died and gone to heaven!* Then it came time to deplane. Kathy took our bags and went out the front door with all the other passengers. I, however, was taken off through the back door of the airplane and put on the same lift used for the airplane supplies. I was lowered to the ground surrounded by toilet paper, cans of soda and cleaning supplies. *Lovely.*

We were excited to get there after almost twenty hours of travel, and the first thing we planned to do was go to the hotel, shower and change out of our gross travel clothes. That was the plan, anyway, until we learned that *none* of our luggage made it. No clothes, no handcycle or racing chair. *Oy.* It was on this trip when we had so many mishaps that we coined the phrase, "It's always something!" Because there was always something to trip us up. At first it was maddening, then funny, then with no clean clothes or racing equipment, we both were on edge. As a schoolteacher, I didn't have much vacation time to use, so it was going to be an ultra-short trip. We flew halfway across the world for a four-day weekend and now we were going to spend most of it wearing the same stinky clothes.

Our luggage and my equipment finally arrived in the afternoon of day two, which was also the day before the race. The course was much more challenging than the Chicago course where I qualified, and I didn't even get the chance to get on my equipment before the race to check it out and loosen up. And all we heard about the water was that it was going to be cold. Very cold.

* * *

On race day, as I dropped gingerly to the ground from my wheelchair and inched on my butt toward the water, my toes were kissed by a small, gentle wave, which sent my usually lifeless legs into a spasm so strong that it nearly knocked me over backwards. The water temperature was below sixty degrees and I had nearly a mile to swim in it.

LakeWakatipu, set in Queenstown, New Zealand, was the race site. As Kathy and I sat next to the lake, tugging and pulling trying to get my wetsuit on, we were surrounded by the other competitors in the physically challenged category (at the time, we were annoyingly called the AWADs—Athletes With A Disability) and in front of us was an expansive, beautiful and very intimidating-looking body of water surrounded by rolling hills that were beginning to show the rebirth of springtime, covered in a carpet of green.

I would be the only athlete in the group who swam backstroke and Kathy would again race with me to steer me in the right direction. Although it was December, and the beginning of summer in this part of the world, both Kathy and I were covered shoulder-to-ankle in wetsuits to retain our body heat in water that had not yet warmed up with the season.

Finally, the horn sounded to begin our race and we set off on a 1.5K-swim, which would be followed by a 40K-bike and a 10K-run. Or, that's how it was supposed to go, anyway.

As we stroked out toward the center of the lake, the full effect of a breezy day kicked in. The waves began to lash out and churn our bodies like clothes in a washing machine. Lying on my back, waves of water constantly crashed over my face, causing me to have to catch small breaths here and there. Not being able to use my legs or the trunk of my body meant that my arms alone were responsible for keeping me afloat and propelling me through the turbulent water.

On my head I had a neoprene cap which had sides that came down over my ears and strapped tightly under my chin like an old-fashioned pilot's helmet. Over the neoprene, I wore a regular latex swim cap. The double layer was to keep my body heat from escaping so that I could retain all of the warmth possible in the frigid temperature of the lake. Unfortunately, the setup did little to help keep in my body heat, but did a more than adequate job of keeping water from escaping my ears, causing it to pool inside my head. The water danced and gurgled throughout the hollow of my ear, causing that echoing deafness which accompanies a congested sinus cavity. Finally, I could no longer hear Kathy and was dependent on her hand signals to continue in the proper direction.

It didn't matter how hard I stroked—I felt like I was on a treadmill, moving constantly, but staying in place. Each time I interrupted my stroke to sit up and look at my surroundings, it felt as if I had been swimming in reverse rather than making forward progress.

It wasn't long before the frustration began to build and billow through my body. It felt like Kathy was constantly yelling "left," "right," "left," "right," I could swear she was leading me on a zigzag course through the water. In reality, I was being tossed around like a rag doll and she had to keep overcorrecting my direction as the waves knocked me off course.

Finally I sat up and found enough breath and energy to yell to Kathy, "I don't think I can do this! How long have we been in the water?"

"You can do this, Trish. Just keep going," she yelled in reply.

"But I'm not getting anywhere!"

"Just keep going!" she yelled.

The debate between us began to heat up just as quickly as our bodies were cooling down. Finally, we started swimming again. But after thirty minutes of being in the water, we weren't even halfway through the course. At my normal pace, I would have been much closer to the finish than to the start, but the waves were unforgiving. My arms began to fatigue and my hands were quickly losing feeling. They got so cold that I could no longer feel my fingers catch the water, and I couldn't provide any resistance to the waves to give me forward propulsion. My thoughts turned negative and berating. Not finishing the race had never been an option in my mind. I had traveled half way across the world. *And for what?* To be flung around for thirty minutes and tossed to the wolves? Those were the animals eating away at my thoughts, my confidence, and my self-worth. "Don't give up," I said to myself, "don't give up, don't give up."

The pain that accompanies extreme cold surged through my hands. My arms were moving, but my body stayed in place. It had become a futile effort. I swallowed what was left of my pride and sat up in the water. I raised my hand, signaling to the rescue boat that my race was over and I needed a lift to shore.

The motor craft pulled up alongside us as two burly sets of arms reached down and pulled me first and then Kathy into the boat. They laid me down and headed toward land. When we arrived at the beach, there were bodies and arms and hands rushing in to get me and carry me to the medical tent. My surroundings were becoming fuzzy and things were happening faster than I could follow. I don't remember my wetsuit being taken off, but soon, I was wrapped in a cocoon of blankets. The medical doctor on staff took my temperature and declared me dangerously close to succumbing to the grips of hypothermia. He called for the ambulance and, like it or not, I was going to the hospital.

The paramedics transferred me to a gurney and lifted me into the back of the emergency vehicle. Looking into the faces of my rescuers, I recognized this sight. My mind flashed back to another day, another place, and a familiar uncertainty about my future. When I got to the hospital, I had a handful of nurses and doctors crowding around my body. They covered me up with blankets and monitored me closely. Lying in the hospital, I felt like I had failed. What should have been the biggest race of my life to that point was a complete bust.

After a couple of hours in the hospital, we were able to get back to the race site to watch our friends and teammates finish. My heart sank as I watched the other athletes cross the line.

Chapter 13

Recovering my life after my injury was not a cut-and-dried process. It was up one day, down the next. There wasn't one day where everything just snapped into place. For me, healing was more of a journey than a destination.

Every year since my accident, I have written a journal entry on New Year's Eve, as sort of a check-in on my progress and my hopes for the new year. Looking back at the first couple of years after my accident, the entries were raw, bitter and pessisimistic. On New Year's Eve 2004, my spirits began to rise. *I am ready to move on, shed the things that are holding me back and open myself up to awesome new things*, I wrote. Little did I know that as soon as I shut that book and made a ten-minute drive downtown, that things would suddenly start to look up.

I was on my way to my friend's house for New Year's Eve

dinner, but I had to make a stop first. I had dropped my handcycle off at the bike shop for a repair and the service manager had called me that afternoon to tell me that it was ready. I didn't want to pick it up on New Year's Eve because I was dressed up and ready to go out, but the shop was going to be closed on New Year's Day and I wanted to have my handcycle since the forecast was for sunny weather.

When I arrived at the shop, the same guy who had called me on the phone was at the counter to help me. He introduced himself as Steve and asked me if he could carry my bike out to the car for me. As we were heading out of the store, I thanked him for working on my bike. That was only the second time I had ever been to that shop, but several local handcyclists had recommended it. Steve apparently had great experience working on adaptive equipment, so I thought I would try it out.

"So how is it that you seem to know so much about handcycles?" I asked him. "Some bike shops don't even want to work on them, yet everyone I have talked to has recommended you as the guy to see."

As we stood in the parking lot right outside my car, Steve explained to me that he had been working with disabled sports programs for more than ten years. He started out as a mechanic for an off-road race team of wheelchair athletes. Then, he got involved in Paralympic cycling and had traveled with the world championship team on several occasions, and just four months earlier, he had been in Greece as the mechanic for the 2004 Paralympic Cycling team. As it turned out, many of the athletes that were on the Paralympic team were the same ones that I had met through my experience as a tandem pilot. We had a whole group of friends in common, yet we had never met. He was so easy to talk to and we had so much in common. We could have talked all evening, but I finally had to excuse myself to head to my dinner.

As I climbed in my car, I couldn't stop thinking about Steve. He seemed so genuine and kind. And he wasn't even fazed by the whole wheelchair thing. When I arrived at my friend's house and he opened the door, he said, "Hey Trish, Happy New Year. How's it going?"

"I just met a cute boy! I think I might like him." And I didn't stop thinking about Steve that whole night.

I wasn't sure how I was going to see Steve again, short of feigning constant flat tires and going in to the shop to buy tubes. But several weeks later when I was having lunch with my friend Terry, we were talking about my training and as luck would have it, she just happened to ask me who I knew that could work on my handcycle.

"Funny you should ask. I just took it to a new shop and this very cute guy did a great job fixing it," I told her.

She asked me who it was and when I told her about Steve, she said matter-of-factly, "Oh, I know him."

"You do?" I asked.

"Yeah, why?" she smiled.

"Well...because I want to go out with him!"

"Oh. Okay. I'll work on that this afternoon." She took

out her Daytimer and made a note of it, like it was a business transaction.

Sure enough, she was good to her word, and Steve took the bait. He called and asked me out on bike ride. We ended up spending the whole day together. After a four-hour ride, we talked for hours over pizza and beer.

Our relationship didn't take off full speed in the beginning. Steve seemed content in his bachelor lifestyle and I was timid about dating after my injury. I was afraid that I would be judged by my appearance instead of who I was. But with Steve, it didn't take long for me to notice that the fact that I was in a chair didn't seem to bother him. In fact, he seemed to take pride in the fact that I was different. Original. He wasn't intimidated by my wheelchair or afraid of what people would think. I liked him because he was so secure and solid. When I would be stressed or worried about something, he would calm me down. If I took something too seriously, he would lighten my mood. I could tell him things I had never told anyone before. And...well, let's be honest, he's a damn good mechanic, and since *everything* I own has wheels, it seemed like a perfect match.

PART III
CHARACTER

"The true test of character
is not how much we know how to do,
but how we behave when we don't know what to do."

—John W. Holt, Jr.

Chapter 14

In 2005, I decided it was time to step up the racing. My life seemed to be falling back into place after the accident and I was ready to challenge myself. I had a new coach named Neal and he was so encouraging and positive that he made me feel like 2005 was going to be an exceptional year. As I sat in his office discussing my training plans and the races I wanted to do, I listed off the marathons, the Olympic distance triathlons, and then I blurted out, "And maybe I'd like to do an Ironman triathlon!" I said it quickly and then held my breath, waiting to see if he was going to laugh me out the door. But he just looked at me, processed what I had said for a bit and then said, "Okay. You'll have to train a lot, but I think you can do it."

An Ironman, or Iron distance, is the granddaddy of all triathlons. It's the biggest, baddest race you can do and all my triathlete friends seemed to be doing them. Not one to be left out, I decided that it was time I try one, too. I had completed a half Ironman in 2004, which is, as it implies, half the distance of the Ironman race. The Ironman consists of a 2.4-mile swim, a 112-mile bike ride and a 26.2-mile run. Aside from the 26.2-mile marathon run, I had never done those other distances since my accident. In fact, the longest I had ever even ridden my two-wheeled bicycle was 107 miles and I remembered how much that had worn me out. I couldn't imagine doing all that all with my arms, but I wanted to try. Neal told me to get online and find a race I could do and he would put together a training plan for me.

It didn't take long before I found a small race, called the Redman, in Oklahoma City. Neal gave me my workouts, which consisted of a steady increase in hours on the bike and the racing chair, and more yardage in the pool. At one point, he told me I was going to have to train for eight to ten hours at a time on my handcycle. I could feel my eyes popping out of my head as he said it, but I wasn't going to give up without giving it my best shot. He taught me how I needed to eat to sustain such a long effort and I did what he told me. I would wake up on a Saturday or Sunday morning, eat breakfast, ride all day, come home, eat and go to bed. My house turned into a pigsty, my social life came to a halt and Steve had to either endure long, slow, boring rides with me, or meet up with me on the couch, when I was beat down and exhausted, to watch movies. He was a great sport even when I offered ideas that were less than appealing.

"Since I'm a little nervous about the Redman, I thought we

could drive to Oklahoma for Labor Day weekend and check out the course," I mentioned off-handedly one day.

"Wow. That sounds like...fun," he said with a sarcastic tone.

"Please?" I gave him my best puppy-dog look.

"Um. Well...okay, but only because I love you."

"You love me *and* you want to go to Oklahoma for a romantic Labor Day trip? This *is* my lucky day!"

The description on the Redman website said that bike course was flat. When we arrived in Oklahoma City, we found something completely different: rolling hills that felt like mountains to me. It did nothing to calm my nerves, but at least I knew what I was up against, so when September 24, came around, I was as ready as I could be.

There are a few things you should know about an Iron distance triathlon. There are these pesky things called time cutoffs. In other words, you can't take two days to do the race. And although the time cuts are basically arbitrary numbers, if you don't finish an event in a certain amount of time, you are taken off the course and not allowed to finish. Most Iron distance races stick to the following cutoffs: two hours and twenty minutes for the swim, 10.5 hours for the swim and bike combined and 17 hours for the entire race. Going into the Redman, I was more confident that I could finish the distance than I was that I could actually make the time cuts.

Because triathlons involve so many details and logistics, there are often pre-race meetings the day prior to the event to make sure that everyone is on the same page. The Redman meeting did a lot to calm my nerves. Roger, the race director, shared with the racers his philosophy about the race. He said there were many first-timers registered and we had all trained hard to be there. He didn't want a time cut to stop the race for anyone. He was not going to stick to the 10.5-hour bike cutoff or even the 17-hour race cutoff. He said if we were still out there and we were going to come in at 21 hours, he would be there at the finish line waiting for us. That was a big relief to me because it meant that the times wouldn't be an issue. Instead, it was up to me and my physical condition as to whether I would cross the finish line or not.

The next morning, my alarm went off at 5 a.m. When I opened my eyes and my brain kicked in, I realized I was about to begin one of the longest days of my life. Looming ahead of me was a 140.6-mile day.

I had all kinds of questions and doubts in my mind that morning. I had never swum a full 2.4 miles in open water. Nor had I ever ridden a full 112 miles on my handcycle. I wasn't sure I deserved to be at the race and my ability to finish was anyone's guess. But, as always, I reminded myself that I needed to remember where I had come from if I was going to be able to appreciate this race, no matter the outcome. I had to remember lying gasping for breath on the pavement after the impact with the car. And remember the day the physical therapists sat me up for the first time in the hospital—the pain, nausea and the lack of balance. That day, I wondered if I would ever be able to sit up again by myself. And I remember when a long ride was four miles through a local Denver park. No matter what happened at the Redman, I'd be miles ahead of where I was five years prior.

As I sat under the moon on the shore of Lake Hefner, in Oklahoma City, Okla., I pulled my wetsuit onto unresponsive legs. With every tug of the neoprene, my thoughts turned to the seemingly insurmountable task in front of me. *What am I thinking? Can I really do this?* Steve kneeled behind me and rubbed my shoulders, whispering encouragement in my ear.

At 7:00 a.m., we got in the water in the dark under the moon. Neal was swimming with me as my guide, but I could barely see him through my goggles because I had dark lenses. I figured the sun had to come up eventually, so I didn't worry too much. When the mass start began, I thought we had gotten mostly to the back, but I found myself running over other swimmers and not being able to find a good space in the pack. I had previously been used to having a lot of room as a back-of-the-pack swimmer, but this time, I was keeping up and even passing quite a few people. Finally, I settled into the swim and tried to concentrate on Neal's hand signals. I was shooting for a 1:40-1:45 swim time, so I knew I would just have to settle in for the long ride. The good thing for me is that I pretty much only have one swim speed. So in this long race, I didn't have to worry if I was going too hard or too slow. I just put it into gear and went. I was almost at the end of the first lap when I felt my neck muscles go. Usually, I swim with my head up just a bit so I can see my guide as I swim backstroke, but I knew there was a good chance my neck muscles wouldn't hold up for that long of a swim, so I

just put my head back—often, with my face totally underwater.
I figured if Neal really wanted me to make a direction shift, he'd
find a way to get his hand right in my face to point which way to
go. I was surprisingly relaxed and kept remembering in my head
the little blue fish, Dory, from the movie *Finding Nemo*..."just
keep swimming...just keep swimming."

Finally, we hit shore at one hour forty-five minutes, and
Steve and Roger rushed in, picked me up and took me to my
chair. I had a group of people gathered around me to take my
wetsuit off and then I was pushed into the changing tent. I was
so lightheaded and foggy at the time that it took everything I had
to stay balanced in my chair and not fall over. I had two women
take off my tank swim top because there was no way I could hold
myself up and change at the same time. The flaps of the tent were
partially open and one woman said to me, "I don't think you're
flashing *too* many people," as she took off my top. I told her I was
pretty sure I didn't care. Then they threw on my cycling jersey
and I was on my way. I got in my handcycle, got my food and
drink and I was off.

The course began by following the dam road that
surrounded the lake, and was the only truly flat part of the
course. That lasted about three miles, and then the fun began.
Heading out to the turnaround wasn't such a bad ride. It was
hilly, but there was an overall elevation loss. As I was going out,
I averaged well over the twelve miles per hour that I needed to
go to stay close to the time cut, so I was feeling good. I had a guy
pass me who said, "You're awesome and you're beautiful!" It made

me smile, and I kept pushing. But as I hit the turnaround to come back, the breeze kicked in and I began climbing. By the time I got to the "Igloo Church"—(there were about nine churches on the course, so we referred to every part of the course by religious landmarks) about 9.5 miles from the transition, my average speed was dropping quickly and I instantly got discouraged. The bike course was a 28-mile loop that you had to do four times, and I was thinking that on lap one I was already down to an 11.9 average, and I still had three more laps to go.

As I got to transition, Steve and Neal were waiting for me, so I smiled as I passed and tried to get psyched for a second lap. I felt okay going out, but coming back, I was starting to not feel so well. My stomach was killing me from all the PowerBars, gels and Gatorade that I was ingesting, it was getting super hot and I was tired of wind and climbing. My average had dropped to just over ten miles per hour.

I pulled into transition the second time not feeling so chipper. I was trying to figure out if it was time to call the race. As I was heading out on the third lap Neal and Steve were standing by the side of the road and I stopped to share with them my thoughts on quitting the race. It was just past 3:00 p.m. and I was thinking that two more laps were going to take six hours or more and it would be past 9:00 p.m. by the time I started the run. I pulled up and shared my time dilemma and asked what they thought I should do. Neal said, "Well, you still have sunlight..." which I gathered meant "stop worrying and keep going." With an accomplished distance athlete as your coach, a little pain doesn't get much attention. So I asked that they keep the van close to me, especially because at the time I felt like throwing up and thought I was going to collapse at any moment. They told me they'd pull ahead and get Steve's bike out so he could ride with me and make sure that I was physically okay. I started feeling more positive about things when Steve was riding with me. (Technically, that's against the rules, but as the only wheelchair racer in the event, it worked out okay.) Besides, at that time, I was one of only a handful of racers left on the course. When Steve was riding with me and I was going back and forth between whining and crying, he said, "If it's your body that's telling you to quit, go ahead, but if it's in your mind, you need to keep going...otherwise, you'll regret it." He was right. I didn't go there to be a quitter and I had to take advantage of the fact that the race director was offering to let everyone finish if they could.

When we arrived in transition at the end of the third lap, Roger was there and I knew we were going to have to have a talk. *Time for the sixty-second pow-wow.* "Are you sure you want to keep going?" he asked me. Everyone was off the bike course at that time and the road was beginning to open up again, and I would be riding with traffic for my last lap. "Plus," he added, "It's starting to get dark." I was beginning to feel his doubts about me finishing and decided that *that* was *not* okay. I can have doubts about my own abilities, but I hate to have other people doubt me, so that got the fire started. I told Roger we'd be fine and said to Steve and Neal, "Let's go!" The guys took a minute to paint the words "Race Support" on the back window of the van and we took

off with Neal driving while Steve and I rode. Neal stayed right
on our tails as Steve and I watched the sun set and rode along
at the best pace I had been on all day. The air got cooler and the
sky got darker. Neal drove between 8-16 mph as we climbed and
descended the rolling hills, following us with headlights glaring so
that we could still see. The bugs were so thick we had to keep our
sunglasses on even though it was dark out. At the intersections,
Neal would check with us to see if we needed water or Gatorade
or gels. My stomach was so mad at me at that point I felt that all
I could handle were gels.

We passed the Igloo Church (9.5-miles down), and then
we passed the Baptist Church. Thankfully! That meant the
turnaround was near. Neal stopped the van with Ozzy blasting
from the speakers. We put on headlights, taillights, made a few
adjustments and we were off on the last leg of the bike. Steve
kept telling me, "You're home free now!" *You know you've had a
long day when finishing a marathon is the least of your worries.*
I knew that it was far from the end, but at least I could get my
head around that and I knew I had it in me to push through.

We pulled up to the Methodist Church, which meant we
were almost there. A quick pit stop and one last gel, and we
started toward transition. Roger met us as we pulled into a
nearly empty transition. Most people were done with the race
and probably asleep in their beds, but it was 9:30pm and I was
ready to do a marathon. My transition was quick and I was off in
the racing chair. Steve led me through the race because it was on
very dark and windy paths through a big park at the edge of the

lake. It was a little dangerous because of the lack of visibility in the dark, but we both had our headlights on and we just put our heads down and were quiet. We were exhausted. I couldn't believe that he had ridden with me the whole time. His jumping on the bike during my ride was an impromptu gesture—he hadn't eaten much before his ride or planned to ride in excess of 80 miles that day, but that was a big sign to me that no matter what, in our lives together, he would go the distance.

When we hit the turnaround, one of the volunteers told us we were on a three-hour pace. I was thinking, *You have got to be kidding! Three hours? I have been going since 7a.m.!* Finally, the mile markers started getting in the twenties and I knew that I was going to be an Ironman. The time was ticking away and I was going to be over the usual seventeen-hour cutoff time, but I was going to make it. Everything I had been through during the day was going to pay off in a completed race. When we saw the big spotlights ahead, Steve pulled off the path and said, "It's all yours." I pushed as hard as I could into the finish. Not that it was a grand finish with hundreds of people watching—there were only a handful of volunteers left—but when I crossed the line at 1:03 a.m., eighteen hours and three minutes after I had begun, I became an Ironman. And there at the end, true to his word, was Roger, waiting to put the finishers' medal around my neck.

I thought I might doubt my status as an Ironman, having missed both the ten-and-a-half and seventeen-hour cutoff marks. But then I remembered the one other runner we passed at midnight. In the pitch black and stillness of the night, I heard his labored breaths as I passed. I could feel the determination oozing out of him and knew that I had the same resolve. I realized then that life is not measured in hours and minutes, but in heart. Right then and there, I knew I had the heart of an Ironman.

* * *

"See what you can accomplish when you're in love?" Terry smiled and said to me as I told her about the Redman over lunch one day. It had been almost a year since she dropped a bug in Steve's ear and told him I wanted to go out with him. "What's on tap for this year?"

"My biggest desires?"

"Yes..."

"A beautiful diamond and a trip to the Hawaii Ironman," I told her and flashed a smile.

"Aaahhh...things are getting serious with Steve, huh?"

I couldn't help adoring him for his kindness and patience and the fact that he put as much faith and effort into my dreams and goals as I did.

Neal and I had been talking about my next challenge since we got back from Oklahoma. I liked the idea of the Iron distance triathlons because, let's face it, I was no spring chicken and my days of sprinting were long gone. I was better at events that required endurance. Also, I liked the idea of doing something original. Since I had started racing, I had met only three other women in chairs who had even done a triathlon, and none of them had done as many as I had. Plus, I figured after all I had endured with my injury, it was going to take something pretty significant to pose a greater challenge than what I had been through in the past five years.

Neal and I got to work making plans and setting goals to get to Hawaii. To get there, I had to complete a qualifier race. Each year, there is one and only one race for a wheeler to qualify for Hawaii. The race is the Buffalo Springs Lake Triathlon, which is a half Ironman. Although I have only done a couple of half Ironman distance races, Buffalo Springs seems to have a reputation of being one of the hardest half Ironman races in the country.

At the end of June 2006, my friend Roberta and I drove to Lubbock, Texas for the race. Steve's schedule wouldn't allow him to join us in the car, but he flew down the night before the race. Our mission was to get me qualified for Kona. Roberta was along as my swim guide and overall support crew.

Race day Sunday started out early, as all triathlons do, with a 3:45 a.m. alarm, a quick pack of the truck and we were off to set up my transition. We unloaded by headlamp and flashlight and were assigned to my handlers. Every wheeler got two handlers for the day—boys (probably high school-age) in a youth corps program, dressed in their army fatigues and following strict orders from the sergeant to not leave their assigned racers. They were at my beck and call, which was quite handy. Once we had everything set up, we headed to the beach to get my wetsuit on, and got ready for the swim.

The race had about one thousand participants, including nine wheelers. There were eight men and me. The guys were going for four slots to Kona and the women had one slot available, so I was fortunate. I was only racing the eight-hour time cutoff on the clock. The guys were chasing the clock *and* each other. From the first moment, I knew I was an underdog, but it wasn't a bad thing because it seemed like everyone was pulling for me. I had all my times planned out. I was shooting for a sub fifty-minute swim, a 5.5 hour bike. That would leave a very tight 1.5-hour for the run (as long as I had quick transition times) and I'd come in with just minutes to spare for the eight-hour cutoff and a trip to Hawaii.

Roberta and I got in the water, and by this race we had swum together enough that we had a groove and were actually quite efficient. Roberta, or Bert, is only pint-sized, but she is tenacious as an athlete, and I knew that her dedication to the swim was as solid as mine was. They announced our wave at 6:35 a.m., just behind the pro wave. The swim went relatively smoothly, but since we were such an early wave, as the other waves of swimmers came up, it caused the water to become choppy and I had a hard time seeing and hearing Roberta's commands. At one point, Roberta had to wave her hands so wildly to make me see, that one of the race rescue kayakers jumped in to save us because he thought she was signaling that we were drowning. Bert is not intimidated in the water and not scared of other swimmers, so there were a couple of times she had to run interference when swimmers got too close, but overall, it was an uneventful swim. When we reached the beach, she said, "Trish! We did that in forty-two minutes!"

When we finished, my handlers swooped in to help me out. They came to the edge of the water, picked me up in a fireman's carry and got me to my chair. One of them had to push me into transition, and he wasn't the greatest wheelchair driver, but he got me there quickly and everyone put in a hand to get my wetsuit off in a hurry. I got settled in on my handcycle and left T1 (the first transition) in just under eight minutes.

The bike leg of this particular race is somewhat deceptive. When you drive into Lubbock, the town is flatter than a pancake, so you think the ride is going to be a cinch. But Buffalo Springs Lake is actually at the bottom of a big canyon and the race goes in and out of this canyon. Leaving the lake on the bike, there are two very steep hills, which are sort of a shock to your system after you've just spent 1.2 miles swimming, and even worse when you're on a handcycle and your arms don't get a chance to rest. I had passed three of the wheeler guys in the swim, but they all ended up catching and passing me on the ride.

Once I got up the first two hills, I was cruising. Anytime time you're not climbing in that race, you're on flats, so my strategy was to maintain high steady speeds on the flats, really crank on the downhills and just settle into a steady, relaxed pace on the climbs.

All was going well until I got to the fifth climb. I was starting to wear down, and this was the climb that really did me in when I had attempted that race, unsuccessfully, in 2003.

Steve and Roberta were following me in the truck, so they stopped
there and walked uphill next to me, trying to keep me focused
and motivated. They said that each time they stopped for me,
they could tell just by looking at my face whether I was enjoying
myself or beginning to hate the sport of triathlon. Over the course
of the day, I went from all smiles, to a frown, to a grimace to full-
on tears.

By the time I reached the seventh climb, I was over it. I
was exhausted, hungry (but my stomach was no longer accepting
food) and hot. I knew I didn't have far, but the last fourteen miles
dragged on and on. On one short stint, I had a tailwind, but it
lasted only about a mile and I was back to steady cross winds.
The last cyclist finally passed me on the course, so it was just me
and the steady hum of my personal follow vehicle's engine. When
we got back to the park where the lake is, I thought I was home
free, although I don't know why. I knew there was a final hill to
climb; after all, I did go down it in the morning. When I got there,
it was like a huge roadblock. I didn't think I could do it. I'm sure
the folks in the follow vehicle didn't think so, either. I climbed at
one mph and stopped every few feet. I was cooked.

I finished the bike in five hours 36 minutes, which
was pretty good and kept me on schedule. But when I got to
transition, I knew I had left every ounce of energy and heart on
the bike course. I pulled into a nearly deserted transition area,
as everyone else was either on the run or finished with the race.
I got to my spot with my everyday and racing chairs and Steve,
Roberta and my two handlers were there to assist. Everyone lent

a hand, but I was so frustrated and exhausted and beyond the point of all reason that all I could say was that I had nothing left and that I couldn't do it. The sergeant, who was there with his youth corps kids (my handlers) came straight up to me, pointed his finger in my direction, and said in a stern voice, "Ma'am, keep your eye on the goal! *Focus* on the goal!" I tried to keep those words with me, but as I pushed out of the transition, I could feel that the time was quickly slipping away.

I got on the run course, which was full of people walking four and five abreast. Since they had finished their races, they were walking their bikes out of the park, taking their picnic chairs and coolers and going home, and I was just beginning. This time, I went out of the opposite side of the canyon from the bike course, but either way you go, it's up. This was probably the steepest hill of the race. Shorter than the bike climbs, but for me, on the racing chair, it was more treacherous. I started out going up faced forward, but realized I was getting nowhere fast and on the verge of tipping over. So I turned around and went up backward. That was getting me a few inches with each pull, but every time I looked behind me at the top of the hill, I didn't feel like I was getting much closer. So I just started to cry. Then I pulled myself together and the cycle started over again. Forward, backward, cry. Forward, backward, cry. I don't know how, but eventually I made it to the top. I looked at my watch. *Maybe I can make this after all.* But then, I hit hill number two—this one not as steep, but longer. At this point, I knew. No eight hours for me. I wanted to turn around and go back. Roberta and Steve were

in the truck following me from behind, and Roberta jumped out
to walk alongside of me. The tears started all over again. I have
never wanted anything so badly, been so close and watched as
it slipped right through my fingers. Roberta, who wanted these
eight hours just as bad, did what any great girlfriend would do.
She cried for me too. "Trish, you've done so well. Eight hours
doesn't mean anything. You have given the best effort you could
and you can't fault yourself for not qualifying. You have given
your best. Just try to make it to the finish." I told her I didn't even
care if I finished. But, even though I wanted to turn around, I
knew I was the only female wheeler in this race, and how lame is
it if you can't win a race when you're the only competitor? Besides
that, I figured if I missed the eight-hour mark, I had all kinds of
time to get to the finish. The course wouldn't close until eight and
a half hours.

Finally, after what seemed like forever, I got to the
turnaround. Six and a half miles is not that far to push in a
racing chair, but it seemed like a marathon in itself getting to
that turnaround. When I finally hit it, I took a deep breath and
headed in. I kept staring at my wrist watching the seconds tick
away. When the stopwatch said 8:00.00, my heart sank. I slowed
my pace, buried my head and just pushed to get to the finish
where I could get in the truck and go drown my sorrows in my
hotel room. On the way back in, I had one more hill to go. At this
point there was a race vehicle in front of me. The driver was full
of spirit and I could tell he wasn't going to let me give up. Every
so often, he'd stop the truck, get out and cheer for me. Jump up

and down. Tell jokes. Anything to get me to smile and push faster. Then he'd get back in and start driving again.

Finally, the finish was around the corner and I heard the announcer say my name. I felt so defeated. I felt like I put in a lot of time, effort, training and money for nothing. It was over—my one and only chance to qualify for my dream race. I kept my head down as I crossed the finish line at 8:29.46.

When I got to transition and got into my everyday chair, Steve came up and put his arms around me. I buried my face in his stomach and sobbed. A few people stopped by my spot in transition and congratulated me on my race and on earning a qualifying slot. Over and over, I accepted the congratulations, but said, "I didn't qualify. I didn't make the eight-hour cut."

After a while, Steve walked to the parking lot to get the car to bring it closer for us to pack my stuff. When he returned, he said, "Trish, they just announced that you made the time cut." I said, "They were just saying that I finished the race before they closed the course at 8:30." But then another racer came over and confirmed what Steve had said. The time cut had been changed to 8:30. I had earned a slot! And I made it by fourteen seconds.

* * *

Buffalo Springs took a lot out of me, but it wasn't rest time when it was over. I had three and a half months to prepare for Hawaii. I came home and took it easy for a couple of weeks, because I had one more race to do before I would make my final training push and then taper for Hawaii.

The New York City Triathlon had been named the National Championships for physically challenged athletes, so that became the next stop on my race circuit. It was my third time to do that race, and the best part about it in 2006 was that there was finally another female wheelchair racer to compete against. I had met April at a couple of marathons in the past, but had never raced against her in a triathlon. In the races we had done previously, we were nearly the same speed. We worked together on the long marathon stretches, drafting off each other. It was no different at the NYC Triathlon. We were neck and neck the whole day. She definitely gave me a run for my money and I only beat her by inches. She was right next to me when I crossed the finish line. It was an exciting victory, which gave me confidence leading up to the Ironman. But that's when things started going wrong. On the airplane on the way home, I started feeling sick. My stomach ached and I was nauseated. When I got home, I went out with friends for the evening, but by the next morning, I couldn't get out of bed. I thought it was just a case of the flu, except I wasn't throwing up and I didn't have diarrhea. In fact, I had the opposite problem. My intestines felt like they had shut down. My energy was gone and I couldn't eat a thing. I would try to get up and do things around the house, but just transferring out of bed and getting a glass of water required a two-hour nap to recover.

I decided to stay in bed and let it pass, but after five days of feeling like I was going to die, and coming just minutes from going to the hospital to check myself in, I decided I needed to do

something about it. Clearly, I didn't have the flu. My friend Amy
worked at an infectious disease clinic and she suggested I come
in and talk to one of the medical practitioners. The woman I
saw suggested that I be tested for parasites, which I might have
picked up swimming in the Hudson River at the NYC Triathlon.
She told me I'd have to produce a stool sample for her.

*Sure. That's a great idea and all, but I can't even produce
one for myself.*

As sick as I was, I felt like I was back at St. Anthony
Hospital. My brother, Greg, was back to asking me every time
he called, "Did you poop yet?" I went to doctor after doctor and
no one could figure out what was wrong. My symptoms didn't
correlate with any of the medical possibilities. I finally started
feeling a little better in August, and I thought I was coming
around. I had barely eaten anything in weeks and was too weak
to even think about working out. I was losing precious training
time for Hawaii, but there was nothing that I could do. My family
suggested that I drop out of the race. But I couldn't get myself to
pull the plug. I even kept my Labor Day weekend plans to fly to
Kona for a course preview and training weekend.

Finally, at the end of August, just before I left for Kona, I
was able to produce the "sample" that the doctor wanted. Steve
had watched a variety of meltdowns at this point and things were
getting stressful. The night before I was to leave for Kona, I was
busily packing my equipment, and trying to pay half attention
to Steve, but my mind was definitely in another place. I knew I
should have been spending time with him because we weren't

going to see each other again for three weeks. The day I was flying home from Kona, he would be flying to Holland with the World Championship cycling team.

As I climbed into bed that night for my four hours of sleep, Steve came to the edge of the bed. He stood over me and said, "You don't have to go through with this, this year, you know? The Ironman will be around next year and the year after that. You're putting yourself through a lot of stress."

"I know, but I really want to go *this* year. I've worked hard for this."

"I know you have, and that's why I will go along with whatever you decide. I promise I will always support you and be there for you." And with that, he got down on one knee and said, "And I don't just mean now or just for this race. I mean...forever." My eyes shot out of my head and my heart pounded in my chest as he unveiled a beautiful diamond ring. He couldn't have picked a better moment to catch me totally off guard, and with that, I said a definite *YES!*

So much for my four hours of sleep.

My friend, Peggy Leigh, and I landed in Kona late in the evening on August 30th and the next morning, my phone rang. It was the doctor's office. "You have giardia," the voice on the other end said. "It's a parasite that usually causes horrible diarrhea, but in your case, it seems to have done the opposite. I can call you in a prescription that you can get started on immediately."

"Yes!" I yelled when I got off the phone.

"What?" Peggy Leigh asked.

"I have giairdia!"

"And this is a good thing?"

"Well, at least now we know what's wrong with me and I can start to get better."

I was so relieved that I wanted to tell everyone who had been as puzzled about my sickness as I had. Plus, I hadn't even had the chance to tell my family yet that I was engaged. So my following conversations went something like this, "Guess what? I got engaged...and I have giairdia!" I was so happy to know what was wrong with me that it seemed perfect to say both pieces of good news in one sentence of excitement.

By the time I got back home, I had only three weeks to work on my fitness before it was time to taper. Before I knew it, I was on my way back to Hawaii.

* * *

Steve and I left Denver and flew to Los Angeles on the Sunday prior to the race. When we arrived in L.A., we decided to get food and some books to read before getting on our flight to Kona. But as we were walking through the airport, we saw a group of people standing around a TV, glued to whatever was happening on the screen. As we got closer, we realized that they were talking about an earthquake that hit Kona. We looked at each other in shock! *Oh no!* We ran to our gate and found that our flight had been cancelled, as well as every other flight out that day. There was a huge line at the counter and we were told that

the holdup was indefinite. No flights would be going to Kona or
any of the other islands for the rest of the day. And, we found out,
it was a slim chance that we could get out the next day. The gate
agents were telling us Tuesday or Wednesday at best.

We headed to the baggage claim and picked up my
handcycle, racing chair, spare wheels and two large bags and had
to get them to a hotel for the night—what was left of it. As we
were leaving the airport, we talked to another airline agent and
told her that we had to get to Kona as soon as possible. She tried
every combination for us and finally came up with a flight that
went from LA to Seattle, on to Maui then, to Honolulu and finally,
Kona. "I know it's a lot of flights, but it's the only way to get you
there before mid-week." We took the tickets and headed to the
hotel for four hours of sleep.

By the time we got to Hawaii, we were spent. We rented
a condo that was mildly accessible rather than choosing a hotel
room, because we were going to have Neal, his wife and their
daughter staying with us. We spent the whole first day going to
the grocery store and the hardware store. We purchased a shower
hose, a plastic lawn chair and a small saw to make my shower
bench. Steve is good about being able to fix, build or create on
the fly, so he sawed off the handle of the chair and put it in the
shower for me. Then, we spent the next couple of days getting
in some workouts and picking up Neal and his family from the
airport.

Saturday was race day and my alarm went off at 3:15 a.m. I
knew that I would be able to tell a lot about how my day would go

just by how I felt when I woke up. I didn't feel so hot. My gut was still feeling the effects of the giairdia, but it wasn't like I could just decide to skip the race, so I did my best to put my worries aside and get ready for a long day.

We arrived at the King Kamehameha Hotel just around 5:00 a.m. for the opening of the transition area. But before you can go into transition where all the bikes and equipment are located, you have to go through the tents at the back of the hotel to be body marked. Neal went with me while Steve parked the car. For body marking at this race, they don't just use a black marker like they do at the local triathlons, but these big block-numbered stamps. My number was 182, and it practically took up my whole bicep by the time they finished stamping it on. They put your number on both arms and then write your age on your calf. Once we were done with that, we were able to go to the transition area.

The physically challenged athletes had their own tent (all other athletes had their bikes racked in the open air). With all thirteen of us and our equipment, it was pretty cozy in our tent—cozy, as in hot, sticky and smelly—like a locker room. Steve and Neal helped me get my equipment set out the way I wanted and then it was time to hang out until the start. Even though I wasn't feeling well, I was trying hard not to show it because NBC was doing a spotlight on me and TV cameras were following me all morning. Finally, 7:00 a.m. rolled around and I had to put on my wetsuit.

The swim was a mass start, so Neal and I got in the water

and found a boat to hang on to until we went off so I wouldn't
have to waste energy treading. The whole cove where the race
starts was surrounded by thousands of spectators. It was truly
a sight. Usually triathlons aren't exactly·a crowd draw. But in
Kona, it's huge.

When we were off, Neal and I took my usual strategy of
starting in the back, but I found again that I wasn't the slowest
swimmer and there were a lot of people swimming behind us. I
did my fair share of clubbing people in the head, but that's what
happens in a triathlon when you're not moving fast enough. I told
Neal that I wanted to do one hour twenty minutes for the swim,
because I knew that with the bike time cut, I'd have to have a
perfect swim *and* a perfect bike to get back to transition by ten
hours and thirty minutes (physically challenged athletes have
the same cutoff times as the able-bodied athletes). I really tried
to motor on the way out to the boat where the turnaround was
located. My arms didn't feel good, but usually it takes a while to
warm up so I kept telling myself to keep moving and eventually
the pain would go away and I'd get into a groove. The waves
tossed me around a bit, and I ingested some salt water going out,
but it didn't seem to be so bad at first. When we got to the boat
to make the turn, we were at 44 minutes. Perfect for me—that
was just right about where I wanted to be, but on the way in,
the waves started to rally. I was swallowing more and more salt
water and was less able to keep my head above where I could
breathe. I couldn't see Neal's hand signals very well anymore and
I felt like I was swimming blindly. My goal was to stop as little

as possible, but every so often my goggles would fill with water and the salt would sting my eyes, so I would stop and hang on to Neal while I cleared my goggles. On the way out, we only had to stop a couple of times, but on the way back in, not only did I have to empty my goggles but the salt water was beginning to make me feel sick, and as the waves picked up I began choking on water. Every time I sat up, it seemed that the shore was getting further away instead of closer and I was being bounced around like crazy. Fortunately, there were several "rescuers" on surfboards, scattered throughout the water. They were there to aid or rescue swimmers. You're allowed to hold on to their boards to grab a rest or catch your breath, as long as they don't give you any forward-moving assistance. There were a few times I knew I needed a longer breath than just having Neal help stabilize me in the water. I kept yelling to the rescue guy to come over to me so I could rest on his surfboard. He later introduced himself as Clint, after I had rested, belched and dry heaved while holding onto his surfboard.

After an hour and one minute, we finished the second half of the swim and Steve and Neal carried me up the stairs from the beach, put me in my chair and started ripping my wetsuit off. We all knew that every minute was going to count in my making the bike cutoff, so I had Steve, Neal and my handler all working to get me ready to go out on my bike. While one person put my socks on, another was slathering me with sunscreen, someone else was putting on my helmet, and in about seven minutes from the time I exited the water, I was off on the bike. (Incidentally, I later learned that this was one of the rougher water swims in Ironman history and that as many as 26 able-bodied racers didn't even make it out of the water before the time cut, so I count the fact that I made it as one of my small race victories.)

I already knew from the moment that I got on the bike that the time cut was probably out of reach. But that still wasn't a reason to abandon the race. You never know what can happen in a race—being faster than expected, a giant tailwind or maybe a miracle. Anything is possible in an Ironman. But as I set off on the handcycle I couldn't seem to get anywhere above six miles per hour. I felt awful. I was thirsty from the salt water, but also had a stomachache and my arms were like rubber. I kept willing my body to pick it up, but it wasn't responding. All I had in my water bottles was sports drink, and I was craving water like never before. I needed liquid, though, so I started chugging the sports drink. *Wrong thing to do.* I could feel it starting to work its way back up, but I didn't want to stop pedaling, so I just leaned over and threw up off the side of my bike while still making forward progress. After throwing up a couple of times, I started to feel better, but I was still fatigued and dying for water. I had the slowest first five miles I've ever had in a triathlon, but after I finished the loop that went through the town of Kona, I headed out on the Queen K Highway, which is where about sixty miles of the bike leg takes place. It's almost a straight shot through lava fields and while the road travels up and down, it's actually an uphill battle. Even when it seems relatively flat you're still going up, which is evident when you're on the return trip and you're cruising.

Traveling along the Queen K was very quiet at first, with just some stragglers passing from behind me every so often, until I got about ten miles into the ride when an NBC car tagged along with me, stopping every so often for a photographer to get out and take some video. Then, it got more interesting when the rain started in and was pouring down, soaking me and making it so I couldn't see out of my sunglasses. I was kind of happy about the break in heat, even though the water on the pavement was slowing me down. Soon, vehicles coming both ways on the road overtook me and a huge helicopter flew super low to the ground just to the right of me. On the nose of the aircraft was this huge camera, and I knew the pros must have been approaching from the opposite direction, heading back to transition. Although I was miles and miles behind them, it was neat to be able to watch up-close as some of the best triathletes in the world passed on the other side of the road.

After about thirty miles, the Queen K ends and you make a left turn onto a short one- or two-mile highway, and then a right turn on the road that leads to Hawi, the course turnaround. Of course, it's not a quick journey to Hawi—it's basically an eighteen-mile climb. Definitely no coasting there. As I neared the turnaround, the winds really picked up and I was getting frustrated, but I kept remembering what everyone had said about the return trip being faster. I was relieved to see the turnaround, but looking at my watch I knew there was no way I was going to make it back before the time cut. On the way back down, I was thinking that maybe I should just flag down a support vehicle to pick me up—I was frustrated and didn't see any reason to keep going. But, I did. Once back on the Queen K, my ride picked up considerably. I was averaging 18-20 mph and had a follow vehicle by that time. When the driver drove up next to me, I asked him if I was going to be swept off the course. He said, "Yes, but I'm not going to be the one to do it, so just keep going and I'm going to follow to make sure you're safe." So I did, and finally started enjoying myself because the ride was so fast and I had gotten my second wind. But, at 10.5 hours, all I could do was wait for the hammer to fall. I kept trying to get as far as I could, thinking that maybe they would give me a break and let me ride all the way in. Better yet, maybe they'd just give me an exception and let me finish the whole race. After all, every racer gets seventeen hours to finish an Ironman. If I just had the chance to finish the bike, I would have been on pace to do even better than seventeen hours, but unfortunately, that 10.5-hour time cut for the bike gets in the way. It's an interesting rule, one that was made for the able-bodied racers, but is enforced on the physically challenged racers too. So where an able-bodied racer only needs to race at an average pace to make the time cut, I have to race at my max, for 8-9 hours (depending on my swim time) to have any chance to squeak in under the time. Unfortunately, at 92 miles, my day was over.

Chapter 15

Over the next two years, Steve and I got married and I gave two more shots at the Ironman. Both times I missed the swim-bike cutoff, and both times I felt a great sense of disappointment. I felt like I had failed myself and those who had helped me along the way. But an email from Neal helped put my shortcomings in perspective.

Neal wrote:

Trish,

Just to reiterate—you are an incredible athlete...and I'm proud that you let me be a part of your successes and risks.

"Our greatest glory is not in never falling, but in rising every time we fall." -- Confucius

Remember—you are your own worst critic...and you need to

be easier on yourself. You do (and have done) amazing things....I believe you beat 20% of the able-bodied field today in the water—if not more! You risked the potential to fall short of your goal, but it is in taking risks that we grow as humans. I know that you can and WILL do anything you set your mind to. For now, though, it's time to put regaining your health as priority number one. Health first, fitness after. Congratulations on stepping up and pushing the envelope—you will breakthrough when the time is right!

"It is not the critic who counts, not the man who points out how the strong (wo)man stumbled, or where the doer of deeds could have done better. The credit belongs to the (wo)man who is actually in the arena, whose face is marred by dust and sweat and blood, who strives valiantly, who errs and comes short again and again, who knows the great enthusiasms, the great devotions, and spends h(er)self in a worthy cause, who at best knows achievement and who at the worst if (s)he fails at least fails while daring greatly so that h(er) place shall never be with those cold and timid souls who know neither victory nor defeat." -- Theodore Roosevelt

Neal

PS—I honestly believe that athletes truly earn their status as an Ironman/Ironwoman in the training that leads up to the race... and you have more spirit of the Ironman than any finisher that I saw out there today.

* * *

In November 2008, I gave the Iron distance triathlon one final try. I headed to Wilmington, North Carolina, for the Beach 2 Battleship Iron distance triathlon. I decided to go to the race for a couple of reasons. First of all, the website said the course was fast and was a great place to set a personal record. The other was that it was a small, low-key, first-year race, similar to the Redman, where I had my first shot of finishing an Ironman in 2005. I had hopes that the race director would allow me to continue through the bike time cut if I was unable to make it. My goal: a chance to cross the finish line, making the bike cut or not.

Steve and I arrived in Wilmington four days prior to the race. I could tell the minute we headed out of the airport that I was in trouble. It was *freezing* outside. Not like Colorado freezing or 32 degrees freezing, but definitely not my idea of triathlon weather. Although I had brought some warm clothes for the race, I wasn't sure I had enough to keep me warm in the current conditions.

We spent Wednesday and part of Thursday checking out the town and the course, trying to figure out the logistics of this somewhat complicated race. There were two different transition areas to locate, the swim was a point-to-point and we had to figure out how everything would happen in between.

On Thursday afternoon, Roberta, my swim guide, joined us in Wilmington, as did my east coast cheering section—my sorority sister, Sandy, and her husband, Marc, kids Kira and Kylan and her Grandma and Paw Paw. We all met for dinner and the last relaxing hours before race day.

By the time I was heading for bed on Thursday, I could feel a slight ache coming on in my throat and the feeling that I was coming down with a cold. I didn't sleep well that night because I kept trying to concentrate on making it go away. No luck. I awoke and knew all my thoughts of keeping it away hadn't worked. But we had a lot to get done, so I sucked it up.

Friday was for last minute equipment adjustments, a short ride and the race briefing. Roberta offered to make our sandwiches that we'd take along for the day, so Steve and I headed out to the parking lot to test out my racing chair and make sure it was working properly. I got in the chair and as I was wiggling down in when we heard a "*THUNK!*" Steve was standing in front of the chair looking at me, and we looked around a second, but didn't really think much of it. Then, Steve walked around the back of my chair to help fasten me in and that's when he said, "Uh-oh."

"Uh-oh what?"

"Um, your frame just cracked."

"Cracked?"

"Yeah, it's snapped."

I tried to give the chair a push on the rims, and I moved forward only about three inches. It was clear then that we had a problem.

I jumped out of the chair and looked down and sure enough, the back of the frame was snapped in half in the back corner. To make things worse, as I had gotten out, I inadvertently dragged my thigh across the jagged edges of the metal. Fortunately, I didn't feel the pain of the eight-inch scrape down my leg. Already stressed and on edge about the race, I took my helmet off, slammed it to the ground and began throwing a tantrum. After screaming, crying and finishing my rant, I yelled at Steve, "What are we going to do now? I didn't train all this time to not race!"

Steve said, "Well, we need a welder."

"How are we going to find a welder?"

I went back to the hotel room and immediately got on the phone. I made calls to see if there might be someone local who could help me out with a chair I could borrow. At the same time, Steve was in the hotel lobby with the phone book, calling local welders. On his third call, he struck gold when he talked to a man named Don who could weld the thin aluminum of my racing chair. Don gave Steve an address and said to come on over.

Steve, Roberta and I piled into the car and started driving. About twenty minutes later, we were in a residential neighborhood. When we came upon the address that Don had given Steve, it was a house with a welding shop in the garage. Don emerged from the shop as Steve unloaded the racing chair. He handed it off to Don and the two of them headed into the shop. Roberta and I didn't even have to get out of the van, we just watched as Don took over and spent less than ten minutes fixing the problem that earlier seemed like the end of the world. He was a nice, no nonsense guy who did us a great favor. Didn't even charge for his work, just said it was great that I could race and good luck.

After that we were back in business, but our running

around didn't give me time for a bike ride, which I had hoped for, so we took the racing chair to our next stop where we would have the race briefing. We put the wheels on the chair in the parking lot and I took a couple of laps to make sure everything was working, and then we went to the meeting.

When we left the meeting, there was still a lot of driving around to do. First, we had to find the beach where the race would start. Then off to T1, where Steve and Roberta would later bring my bike, then back to the hotel so I could get my things together. I had a quick dinner and was in bed by 8 p.m. since we had to leave the hotel by 4:45 a.m.

Race morning was chilly and dark. I was full of dread. My cold had me feeling less than ideal, and I was anxious about the day. Steve, Roberta and my friend Sandy and I piled in the van and headed to T1 to drop off my special-needs bags and then headed to the beach. While all the other racers had to take a bus from T1 to the beach since there was little parking there, we got a special "P.C." parking pass and could drive ourselves. As the busses arrived, the athletes had piled out and stood shivering in the cold waiting for race time. All the while, we had the heat cranked in the van and we sat in there relaxing.

When we headed for the beach, Steve and Roberta started to carry me in a fireman's carry, but we soon learned that it was about a quarter-mile walk to get to the edge of the water. Steve ran back and got the van and four-wheeled across the sand, picked us up and dropped us at the water's edge.

I don't know what the worst part of the Ironman is. When

I think about it, I think each of the events overwhelms me in its own way. For me, the swim is stressful with the waves and other racers crowding me and not being able to see my way along the course. The bike is long and causes a great deal of anxiety because of the time cut. The run, if I make it that far is, well, a marathon. I knew I was in for another very long day.

The one thing this swim had going for it was that it was in salt water, but instead of being an ocean swim, it was actually in a protected channel. And, we would be swimming with the tide. They said it would be fast and I was hoping that was true. The other good thing about the swim was that it was a straight shot, point-to-point. For some reason, that seems to be better for me. Also, not having the waves I had to fight in Hawaii, I was able to lie back and relax. I only had to stop three times during the whole swim, which is a record for me. One time was because I couldn't figure out what Roberta was trying to tell me, and the two other times, I had to clear my goggles because I had salt water in my eye. Each time, Roberta would tell me my time and it would give me more motivation because we were going so fast. I couldn't believe when we reached the finish and we had done a 1:10! Steve was at the dock along with a couple of other guys, to pull us out.

Then we had to get across the street to the transition. Toward the end of the swim, my hands were cold and I was unable to keep my fingers together on my right hand to catch the water very well, but I didn't realize until I got in the changing tent just how frozen my hands were. The air didn't help, because it wasn't warm either. I couldn't do a thing for myself. My hands weren't responding. Roberta literally stripped me naked, put on my jog bra, my long-sleeved shirt, jersey and socks. All I did was try to hold myself up. Then, she pushed me to my bike and she and Steve got me ready to go and saw me off.

Too bad that what I saved in swim time, I sucked up in transition time, but I still had nine hours to do the 112-mile bike course, so I pushed on. As I was peddling with hands I could barely feel, I was trying to figure out how best to get through the beginning of the ride. I started blowing on my hands through my gloves, but that wasn't warming them. Then I thought I could stop and try to warm them up on the pavement. I tried to wiggle my fingers—anything to get the circulation going. I tried to reach into my food bag to get a gel, but when I clenched my fingers together and pulled them out of the bag, I realized they didn't pick up anything. I tried again and again and couldn't get them to grasp anything. I started thinking of my right hand as "robot hand" because it was like it wasn't even connected to my body. Since that wasn't working, I decided to concentrate on keeping my speed up, and although I couldn't get a good grip on the pedals, my speed was okay, so I wasn't too concerned about my progress.

After an hour, I could finally feel my fingers and get some food into my body. My speed was under control and I was still with the field of the half Ironman racers who had started behind us, so I wasn't on the road alone. After a couple of hours, though, the other racers thinned out and then, finally, were gone. It wasn't a first to be on the a race course alone, so it wasn't so bad until I got to a fork in the road where I wasn't sure which way to go on the poorly-marked course. Even though we had driven the route a couple of days before, the map on the website was vague and we ended up missing several roads.

I started to make a turn and then decided against it, then went up the road, then turned around and turned around again. I began to panic! I was on my time schedule and knew I didn't have time for mistakes. Finally, I decided to go with my gut, but I kept watching the ground for empty gel packs, water bottles—anything that would signify that the riders had followed this road. Eventually, I saw a clearing in the woods that I remembered driving by with Steve, so I began to relax. But by hour three of riding into a breeze, up some slight grades, and beginning to tire, my speed was slowing below where it needed to be. I was frustrated.

I was wondering where Steve, Roberta and Sandy were in the van and I was starting to get bummed that my day was going downhill.

By about fifty miles, the van showed up and my support crew jumped out and cheered for me. As I rode by, I warned them that I was off pace and I wasn't going to make it. In the back of my mind I was still hoping for a massive tail wind for my way back to transition, but I knew it would take a slight miracle to make it in 10:15 (this time cut was fifteen minutes faster than the other races I'd done).

As I passed my crew, there was another fork in the road and I began to ride straight along the road. Behind me they said, "Take a right here, Trish!"

I was skeptical. "Are you sure?" I asked.

"Yes!" they yelled.

So, I took a right.

Wrong! Now I wasn't just frustrated or bummed. I was *mad*! I was mad about being off course, I was mad at the crew's wrong call, I was mad about the lack of course markings, I was mad about being slower than I needed to be. I threw my water bottle down at the ground, flung my food across the road, yelled, screamed and threw a tantrum. How could everything about this race be so frustrating!

That was the beginning of the end. Once back on course, mentally I was broken down. I was over it. The day wasn't going where I had anticipated and I didn't want to be out there. Unfortunately, I had a good five hours left of riding. I pulled over and told the crew I was quitting the race.

"Don't do that—you'll regret it," they told me. I kept going.

At some point, we had another support vehicle from the race start traveling with us. Two volunteers drove in a truck in front of me, while Steve, Roberta and Sandy trailed me from behind.

Even with all the support, I tried to quit again. No sympathy. So I said, "Fine. I'll keep going if you call the race director and make sure that I'm not going to get pulled from the course at the time cut or kept from doing the run." They called and confirmed. I had the green light.

At this point, there was not a positive thought going through my head. I was mad at everyone in the van behind me. I was mad at the road in front of me.

Finally, I thought, *Really, I am quitting! I don't care about this anymore!* When the crew got out to see why I had stopped, I could feel a blanket of guilt suffocate me. Like I was going to let everyone down if I quit. I know they worked hard to get me there, but I wasn't feeling support at this moment from my crew. I rode off without saying anything.

Fine. I'll do it, I thought. *But don't expect me to be nice about it.* I just kept my eye on my front support vehicle and wondered what drove them to want to stay with me for four hours at ten miles per hour.

Whenever they asked me anything from the van, or when they stopped to give me warm clothes, I gave one-word answers, if I said anything at all. I was pissed off and wanted them to know it.

After ten hours and twenty minutes on the bike (and almost twelve hours after the race had started), I pulled into T2. This was another fiasco, as I still did not want to go on and I couldn't get squeezed into my racing chair because I was so sweaty and sticky. I finally got in my racer, but was sitting totally crooked. I couldn't get straight and settled in comfortably, and I still had 26.2 miles ahead of me to push.

I headed off. *I'll do one lap*, I thought. As I left transition, Steve, Roberta and Sandy were there cheering me on my way. In the back of my head, I knew I should just suck it up, but I was in a bad mood that couldn't be broken.

It was dark and there were still runners on the course. I slowed to talk to a few and told myself if I could find one person who was still on his or her first lap like I was (the run course was two laps), then I would stick it out. But each person was on the second loop. *Great.*

We hadn't pre-driven the course and I thought it was supposed to be flat. I climbed up and over two bridges and then hit a hill downtown that was so steep I had to go up backwards. Then I started settling in a little, but there were so many turns and I was still so mad, I wasn't doing myself any favors. Finally, after much longer than I had planned, I finished my first lap.

As I set out on my second lap I started to pick it up a little, but as I crossed the first bridge, I realized the lighted arrows that marked the course had been taken down. Although the seventeen-hour time cut had not yet expired, they had figured that no runners should just be starting their second lap, so they started taking down the course. They obviously had forgotten about the lone wheeler out there.

The run course was dark. And empty. No people anywhere. I was scared and thought I had better just turn around. It didn't strike me as being safe to head out in a town I didn't know, that wasn't well lit and with turns on the course that I didn't know or remember from the first lap.

Fortunately, I had paid just enough attention to some random curbs, potholes, and turns to remember the beginning of the course, but I knew I better hustle because once I got to the park, I would be out of luck if the arrows were all gone. The park we went through was pitch black and was more like a forest with a winding path through it, and there was *no way* I could remember the course. About mile four or so of my lap, I saw a police officer and asked him if he had communication with the race director or anyone who could alert the marshals and aid stations to keep the course open. He didn't, but he said, "I'll follow you the whole way until you get to the finish."

I took off at *full* speed and chased down the course. Once I got to mile six or seven, there were still some remnants of the course, but when I got to the park, there was a curb that I had to get over. On the first lap there were volunteers there to help me, but this time, there was no one. I turned around to find that even the policeman wasn't behind me. At this point, I started to get angry again. *I have come so far and now this!*

Just then, my escort pulled up and got out of the car. I asked him to get me over the curb, so he did and I took off. He couldn't follow me on the path, but he could keep an eye on me as he drove the perimeter road.

By the time I got to about mile 23, I saw a few straggling runners, so I knew I'd be able to find my way to the finish. The officer followed me up and over the final bridge and then pulled off as I headed toward the line.

It wasn't the grandest finish line crossing because I was still feeling sour from the day, but it was a victory for my support crew, who were all excited when I crossed the line at sixteen hours and twenty minutes. I may not have made the bike cut, but I did make the seventeen-hour overall time, which was better than my eighteen-hour performance at the Redman three years prior.

It took until our van pulled up in the hotel parking lot that I was ready to say a word to my support crew. I was grateful to have had such a dedicated crew, but I wondered, *Is it possible that they were just a little too supportive?*

The truth is, they know me. They knew that if I didn't make the bike time cut, my goal was to finish an Ironman in under seventeen hours. They know how disappointing a DNF (did not finish) is and how you can never go back and change it.

One of my biggest pet peeves is people who think they know me better than I know myself. Fortunately or unfortunately, my support crew thought they knew what was best, and the amazing part was that they were actually right. I will not say that was one of the best races of my life, but it was truly a test. And it was a test for everyone involved. It took mental, physical and emotional strength for all of us to get through the race. I might have been the one who physically crossed the finish line, but I didn't earn the medal. That one was for my support crew. Without them, I would have hung it up at 56 miles of the bike. Thank goodness not only for those we love, but for those who truly love us back!

PART IV
HOPE

"Hope is the thing with feathers, that perches in the soul,
and sings the tune without words, and never stops at all."

—Emily Dickinson

Chapter 16

My road to recovery was a lot like my final Ironman.
There were times it seemed absolutely impossible, and days
when I didn't want to go on. I screamed and cried and cursed my
situation. But there were so many people around me who stood
by and let me have my time to grieve while gently nudging me
forward. It has been, and sometimes continues to be, a mountain
to climb. As someone once told me, the journey to healing is a
marathon, not a sprint. It doesn't change or fix itself overnight.
It takes hours, days and years of work. It takes waking up every
morning with a fresh sense of optimism that things *will* get
better.

On September 17, 2009, I loaded my handcycle in the back
of my car and drove to Lookout Mountain. As I peddled with my
arms up the road toward the summit, a million memories came

rushing back into my mind. Nine years earlier, this had been my last ride as an able-bodied athlete. I remembered the feeling of power and freedom that my bicycle gave me. I felt so strong, I thought I might be invincible. I have learned now that I am *not* invincible and that life cannot be taken for granted—I appreciate each and every day unlike ever before. But I've also learned that I am a lot tougher than I knew, and inside me burns a fire that is not easily dampened. Life is full of tests and obstacles. There is never a free ride. But even though things get hard and life can feel like a series of uphill battles, I now remind myself: there is always *Hope*.

Acknowledgements

The hardest part of writing is knowing where to begin and getting the first words on paper. I am thankful to have had the guidance of Lynn Dean, who helped me launch this project. Our conversations, as well as her help in interviewing family members about those first dreadful days after the accident, set the stage for my writing and allowed me to take the story and run.

I appreciate the encouragement from Melissa Taylor and Jane Nyman, who assured me that I could, in fact, write this story. I couldn't have done without Jane's guidance through my phone calls, emails and panic attacks. Thanks to Beth Kenny, Amelia Reinkensmeyer, Pecanne Eby, Tracey Karczewski and Mom for reading the early drafts.

Thank you to the following people for their professional help: Mark Woolcott, photography; Stacey Lane, cover design;

Stephanie Chandler and Amberly Finarelli, publishing. Also to Sara Baum, Polly Letofsky, Claire Brown, LeAnn Thieman, Beth and Jane for creative input and moral support.

Thanks to the care and encouragement I received from St. Anthony Hospital, Craig Hospital and support for my sports endeavors from the Challenged Athletes Foundation.

I am thankful to my parents for instilling in me the value of never giving up, my four brothers Sam, Andy, Greg and James, who all played a role in my healing, and the rest of my family and friends who saw me through a very difficult time in my life.

Finally, a deep gratitude to Jack, my kitten, who sat on my desk (and sometimes on my keyboard) for most of the hours I spent writing this book, and for my loving husband Steve, who supports and encourages me, and who has more faith in me than I have in myself.

Without all of these people, I wouldn't have gotten to where I am today. But with them, I have a story to tell and one that has a happy ending.

Tricia Downing

Tricia Downing is recognized as a pioneer in the sport of women's wheelchair triathlon. She has competed in the sport both nationally and internationally, in addition to competing in marathons and duathlons. She was featured in the Warren Miller documentary *Superior Beings* and on the lifestyle TV magazine show *Life Moments*. She has been featured in *Muscle and Fitness Hers*, *Mile High Sports* and *Rocky Mountain Sports* magazines.

Tricia is the founder and director of Camp Discovery, a fitness camp for women in wheelchairs designed to promote health and healing on all levels—mind, body and spirit. She holds Masters degrees in both sport management and disability studies and is a motivational speaker.

She lives in Denver, Colorado with her husband Steve. Visit Tricia at trishdowning.com